ॐ

SRI YANTRA BHAVANA
UPANISHAD

Essence and Sanskrit Grammar

भावनोपनिषद् (श्री चक्रोपनिषद्)

bhāvanopaniṣad (śrī cakropaniṣad)

Ashwini Kumar Aggarwal

जय गुरुदेव

Title: **Sri Yantra Bhavana Upanishad**
SubTitle: **Essence and Sanskrit Grammar**
Author: **Ashwini Kumar Aggarwal**

Printed and Published by
Devotees of Sri Sri Ravi Shankar Ashram
34 Sunny Enclave, Devigarh Road,
Patiala 147001, Punjab, India

https://advaita56.in/
The Art of Living Centre
https://www.artofliving.org/

21st June 2023, International Day of YOGA, Prime Minister
Narendra Modi leads historic Yoga Session with President of UN
General Assembly Csaba Korisi, Deputy Secretary-General Amina
Mohammed, and NY City Mayor Eric Adams at UN Headquarters in
Manhattan New York.

Guinness World Record for most nationalities in a Yoga session where people
from 135 Nations took part. Summer Solstice. Ashadha Shukla Tritiya, Pushya
Nakshatra, Grishma Ritu, Uttarayana.
Vikram Samvat 2080 Pingala, Saka Era 1945 Shobhakrit
1st Edition June 2023
जय गुरुदेव

Dedication

Sri Sri Ravi Shankar

who taught us Mother divine worship, Old Meditation Hall
below Sumeru Mantap, Navratri Oct 2003, Bangalore
Ashram

Acknowledgements

Padmasadhana 3 rounds on The Ridge Shimla at the
Lookout adjacent to Himachal Pradesh State Library, over
Gandhi Statue, facing the National Flag. IDY 2023.

Blessing

Yoga is not just a set of stretches but an attitude –
How you care for Nature,
How you connect with people
        of all races, cultures and religions.
That oneness with Divinity, with Nature and People,
        is the real essence of Yoga!

                                        Sri Sri Ravi Shankar

https://www.facebook.com/photo/?fbid=10158438647822536

https://twitter.com/SriSri/status/543775429325119489

Yoga: A Science for World Peace. 4-5th Dec 2011, Vishalakshi Mantap, Bangalore Ashram

https://yensures.com/2023/06/20/international-day-of-yoga-the-background/

Photo courtesy Guru Puja Havan 10 March 2014 Patiala

Preface

Adi Shankaracharya's masterly commentary on eleven Upanishads is the de facto standard for Vedanta. These eleven have been named the principal Upanishads. Though it is said there are 1180 Upanishads written over a period of a thousand years, actual manuscripts available as of now are 108 only.

A chart that lists the eleven Upanishads commented on in detail by Sankara.

Rigveda	Samaveda	<u>Shukla Yajurveda</u> Krishna Yajurveda	Atharvaveda
Gives the fundamental laws of creation	Gives the intrinsic harmony within creation	Gives the specific design, administrative and governing principles for a family or a nation	Gives the specific ritucharya and dinacharya for an individual
Aitareya	Kena **Chandogya**	Ishavasya **<u>Brihadaranyaka</u>** Katha Taittiriya Shvetashvatara	**Mandukya** Mundaka Prashna
प्रज्ञानम् ब्रह्म	तत् त्वम् असि	अहं ब्रह्म अस्मि	अयम् आत्मा ब्रह्म

Four great illuminating statements or mahavakyas are listed above with their corresponding Upanishads in **bold**.

Vedic Sanskrit can never be adequately
translated. It has sutras and dictums that
can each form an entire school curriculum.
The only way is to wait until words and
sentences sprout after deep meditation in the
presence of an enlightened master.

The Sri Yantra Bhavana Upanishad is attributed to the
Atharvaveda. It is a later Upanishad that illuminates the
Bhavana or **Deeper Emotions** connected to the Sri Yantra,
the body of the Mother Divine, and also the body of Divine
Yogic Union of Purusha and Prakriti.

It expounds the innermost intense feelings of the Soul, its
basic desire, and ways and means to connect and unite with
the ultimate consciousness.

In this text, Sri Chakra and Sri Yantra are synonyms. The
Wheel of Life is properly grasped by a physical constructed
Yantra that deciphers the Purpose of Life.

Contents

Prayer

ॐ

भ॒द्रं कर्णे॑भिः श‍ृणु॒याम॑ देवाः । भ॒द्रं प॑श्ये॒म अ॒क्षभि॒र्यज॑त्राः ।
स्थि॒रैरङ्गै᳚स्तुष्टुवाꣳस॒स्तनू॒भिः । व्य॑शेम दे॒वहि॑तं॒ यदायुः॑ ॥
स्व॒स्ति न॒ इन्द्रो॑ वृ॒द्धश्र॑वाः । स्व॒स्ति नः॑ पू॒षा वि॒श्ववे॑दाः ।
स्व॒स्ति न॒स्ता॒र्क्ष्यो॒ अरि॑ष्टनेमिः । स्व॒स्ति नो॒ बृह॒स्पति॑र्दधातु ॥
ॐ शान्तिः॒ शान्तिः॒ शान्तिः॑ ॥

Shanti Mantra of Atharvaveda

O Divine Wisdom!
May our ears listen to the sacred and the auspicious.
May our eyes see the propitious as we come together to
partake of wisdom.
May our limbs be firm and body attuned to long endurances.
May our senses function with full alertness and
May the sense of contentment be strong.
May our good thoughts form a discus to shield us, and
May our education give us a shining personality.

Peace in our heart, in our body and in our environs.

Introduction

What is a Sri Yantra? A healing mandala diagram made by 4 Upward Apex Triangles and 5 Downward Apex Triangles, properly intertwined to represent
- the cosmic forces in creation, and
- the principles of duality, harmony, and divinity.

The 9 Basic Triangles create a total of 43 Triangles due to the overlapping, which are grouped (shaded) as
$14 + 10 + 10 + 8 + 1 = 43$.

Apart from these Triangles,
- there is a central Dot (Bindu)
- there are three Circles encircling the Triangles
- there are four Gates encircling the entire Mandala, composed of three lines.

Sanskrit Seed Sounds (bija mantra) like ॐ Om, are potent healing and nourishing energies. Sound is an energy. Pleasing sounds (meditative music, blessings) have excellent effects on one's behavior, attitude, and long-term all round success in life.

An aesthetically made Mandala can become vastly superior when infused with Seed Sounds.

॥ ॐ श्री ललिता महात्रिपुरसुन्दर्यै नमः ॥

श्री यन्त्रम्

In Sanskrit we use the **feminine** spellings for the directions and the divinities.

पूर्वा, ईशानी, उत्तरा, वायव्या, पश्चिमा, नैर्ऋत्या, दक्षिणा, आग्नेयी ।

पूर्वा East, ईशानी NorthEast, उत्तरा North, वायव्या NorthWest, पश्चिमा West, नैर्ऋत्या SouthWest, दक्षिणा South, आग्नेयी SouthEast.

Bhāvanopaniṣad भावनोपनिषद्

अथ भावना – उपनिषद् atha bhāvanā - upaniṣad

Now begins the Bhāvanā

Vowel Sandhi – Guna Sandhi – अ + उ → ओ

भावना + उपनिषद् → भावनोपनिषद् ।

Bhavana means deep emotion. Highly Meditative state.

Soul's Yearning. Heart's Contemplation.

Qualifications Prerequisites

The Upanishad is a masterly text, meant for a sincere and serious aspirant. Basic qualifications include a command over language, cleanliness, and neatness in attire.

Other qualifications most essential to imbibing the knowledge are:
- Respectfulness
- Readiness to serve with cheerfulness
- Capacity to maintain discipline for a year with frugal lifestyle
- Truthfulness and candor in communication

Painting courtesy TOK Punjab Nov 2010 Ludhiana

Guru Parampara

ॐ आत्मानम् अखण्ड-मण्डलाकारम् आवृत्य सकल-ब्रह्माण्ड-मण्डलं
स्वप्रकाशं ध्यायेत् । श्री गुरुः सर्वकारणभूता शक्तिः ॥ १ ॥

oṃ ātmānam akhaṇḍa-maṇḍalākāram āvṛtya sakala-
brahmāṇḍa-maṇḍalam svaprakāśam dhyāyet |

śrī guruḥ sarvakāraṇabhūtā śaktiḥ ॥ 1 ॥

The Guru is the primary mover and cause of this entire
creation. From him is illumined the entire cosmos. He shows
the path to whosoever has sincere devotion. He guides
towards bliss and final enlightenment.

Divine Yogic Union of Purusha and Prakriti

तेन नवरन्ध्ररूपो देहः ॥ २ ॥

tena navarandhra-rūpo dehaḥ ॥

तेन नव-रन्ध्र-रूपः देहः ॥

तेन ^{mfn3/1} by that (soul) नव-रन्ध्र-रूपः ^{m1/1} nine-avenued-form देहः ^{m1/1} body ॥

In this verse the number nine does not mean the physical number 9. Rather it is points to an infinite yearning using the math $3x3 = 3^2$.

The word aperture does not simply mean socket or opening, rather it points to modes of communication, expression, various ways of doing something, looking at the same thing from another angle,

Endless possibilities in short.

3x3 = 9 = Diverse Avenues Expressions

2. By the supreme consciousness, the best body manifested in creation has 9 apertures. Body simply means Tool to achieve a specific task. An instrument needed to do a particular job, and once it is done, the instrument is shelved, put away, not needed. Why is the nine-faceted tool considered the Best? Each aperture signifies an important facet or quality.

Here the math goes like 0, 1, 3, 3x3 = 3^2 = 9, ...
0 = undifferentiated consciousness. A pool of life. A band of energy.
1 = this pool is now equipped with eyes, i.e., the faculty to sense itself or know own presence / existence is available.
3 = a balancing grid, triad, or foundation is now apparent. Usually called Sattva Rajas Tamas. Winter Summer Monsoon. Centered High Low. Gold Silver Bronze. Sunrise sunset sandhya. Masculine Feminine Neuter.
3^2 = 9. After the basics are in place, an exponential explosion happens. A leap to infinity is envisaged. The squaring is just a symbol, the smallest easily understood method for teaching expansion, growth, evolution, success, target or personal goal. After life gets born, and the baby's body and intellect become fully formed, at age three or thereabouts, it is time to tell him - mate you have to reach the stars. You are born for a great noble purpose. Make Honesty Hard work Patience as your defining limits, and go on to achieve the impossible, go on to do what no one has so far even thought or imagined. Life is big, very big, Time Space Consciousness are just about infinite from every conceivable and inconceivable angle. And YOU must stretch your wings and go far, leaving behind your comforts, family, and everything else.

नवशक्तिरूपꣳ श्रीचक्रम् ॥ ३ ॥

nava-śakti-rūpaꣳ śrī-cakram ॥

नव-शक्ति-रूपं श्री-चक्रम् ॥
नव-शक्ति-रूपं $^{n1/1}$ 9fold-energies-form (signifying) श्री-चक्रम् $^{n1/1}$
the Sri Chakra (is) ॥

9 = Infinity expressed by Inscribed Sri Chakra

3. Sri Chakra is that which has the aforementioned 3x3 = 3^2 = 9 forms, angles, expressions, vibrations.

A Sri Chakra is endowed with innumerable energies. It is impregnated with seed sounds carrying immense shakti.

When a Sri Yantra is manufactured with Sanskrit Seed Sounds printed on it, it automatically gets endowed with immense potential for all round good.

वाराही पितृरूपा । कुरुकुल्ला बलिदेवता माता ॥ ४ ॥

vārāhī pitṛrūpā | kurukullā balidevatā mātā ||

वाराही पितृरूपा । कुरुकुल्ला बलिदेवता माता ॥ ४ ॥
वाराही [f1/1] Feminine aspect of Varaha Avatar पितृ-रूपा [f1/1] lineage of ancestors । कुरु-कुल्ला [f1/1] field of energy बलि-देवता [f1/1] ready for sacrifice for another - light being माता [f1/1] mother ॥

माता mother divine. That loving presence which rejoices in each expression of ours. No matter what we do or say or do not do, she loves it, applauds, and is watching. Available. Total Protection.

Inscribed Sri Chakra represents Completeness

4. Let us separate the letters in this verse.

Distinct Vowels आ ई इ ऋ ए अ उ ।

Semivowels व र ल ।

Nasals म ।

Row consonants प त द् क ।

Sibilants ह ।

Conjunct ह्ल ।

<u>Independent words</u>

वराह varaha avatar that which lifts out of gloomy obvilion and brings forth to brilliant light and freedom. पितृ pitr lineage of ancestors, the cause for one's life. देवता devata means a light being, a bodiless energy form, something that is unrestricted, unbound by space and time. That on which the physical and chemical laws of nature do not operate. Beyond the laws of embodied beings. कुरु kuru is the domain of expression. The playground. The field where we exhibit our talent, the platform where we perform. The area that is governed by the laws of space and time. Where nature, environment, weather, terrain all are strongly felt and have a definite say on performance. कुल्ला kulla is the principle of nourishment, support, or that energy which shall work in our favor, and help keep our strength and wits.

पुरुषार्थाः सागराः ॥ ५ ॥

puruṣārthāḥ sāgarāḥ ॥

पुरुषार्थाः सागराः ॥
पुरुषार्थाः [m1/3] Goals of Emancipation सागराः [m1/3] deep waters
/ infinite emotions ॥

Infinite are the Aspirations and Goals

5. As pervasive, deep, and mysterious the Oceans are, so too our aims, expectations, desires, fancies and their physical outcomes in the form of words and deeds and strenuous efforts.

Generally, the efforts of mankind are directed towards four distinctly classifiable objectives, viz Artha Kama Dharma Moksha or Sustenance, Entertainment, Social empowerment, and Self Liberation.

The Upanishad here says –
How men go about fulfilling these four broad aims is as diverse and mysterious as the oceans.

- The same task is solved differently,
- the same city is approached variously,
- the same grain is cooked and deliciously spiced to satisfy so many different palates.

देहो नवरत्नद्वीपः । त्वगादिसप्तधातुभिः अनेकैः रोमसंयुक्ताः ॥ ६ ॥

deho nava-ratna-dvīpaḥ | tvak-ādi-sapta-dhātubhiḥ anekaiḥ saṃyuktāḥ ॥

देहः नव-रत्न-द्वीपः । त्वगादिसप्तधातुभिः अनेकैः रोमसंयुक्ताः ॥

देहः [m1/1] embodied being नव-रत्न-द्वीपः [m1/1] 9 gemstones island । त्वग्-आदि-सप्त-धातुभिः [m3/3] with skin-etc-7-tissues अनेकैः [adj3/3] with many रोम-संयुक्ताः [m1/3] hair attached ॥

Infinite Embodied Beings

6. Nine avenues to blossom and achieve success for the structure fortified with 7 specially formulated tissues, except for skin that tingles with soft lush glossy hair.

Notice here 9 means 3x3 = 3^2
i.e.,
a mathematical device to say diverse ways.

Just as we say there are 9 (approachable and livable) planets, but we actually mean there are billions of stars for us to travel to and do work of our choice.

The internal structure of anatomy is hinted at here. It consists of 7 tissues, apart from **skin** that has **hair** attached to it, making 9 tissues in all.

The 7 tissues that constitute a human body are:
Rasa, Rakta, Mamsa, Medha, Asthi, Majja, Shukra.
- Plasma and hormonal Fluids
- Blood
- Muscles
- Fat
- Bone
- Bone marrow
- Sperm and virile tissue

सङ्कल्पाः कल्पतरवः । तेजः कल्पकोद्यानम् । रसनया भाव्यमाना मधुराम्लतिक्तकटुकषायलवणरसाः षड् ऋतवः ॥ ७ ॥

saṅkalpāḥ kalpataravaḥ ॥ saṅkalpāḥ kalpataravaḥ । tejax kalpaka-udyānam । rasanayā bhāvyamānā madhuḥ-āmla-tikta-kaṭu-kaṣāya-lavaṇa-rasāḥ ṣaḍ ṛtavaḥ ॥

सङ्कल्पाः कल्पतरवः । तेजः कल्पकोद्यानम् । रसनया भाव्यमानाः मधुराम्लतिक्तकटुकषायलवणरसाः षड् ऋतवः ॥

सङ्कल्पाः $^{m1/3}$ intentions कल्प-तरवः $^{m1/3}$ wish fulfilling trees तेजः $^{m1/1}$ mind's glowing energy कल्पक-उद्यानम् $^{n2/1}$ fanciful garden (is as if) । रसनया $^{f3/1}$ by the tongue भाव्य-मानाः $^{m1/3}$ benevolent thoughts मधुः-आम्ल-तिक्त-कटु-कषाय-लवण-रसाः $^{m1/3}$ sweet-sour-pungent-bitter-astringent-salty tastes षड् $^{mfn1/3}$ six ऋतवः $^{m1/3}$ seasons ॥

कल्पतरवः from कल्पतरु । भाव्यमानाः from भव्यमनस् । ऋतवः from ऋतु ।

By Sandhi भाव्यमानाः मधुराम्लतिक्तकटुकषायलवणरसाः → visarga drops → भाव्यमाना मधुराम्लतिक्तकटुकषायलवणरसाः ।

Infinite Aspirations All Fulfilled

7. Fancies Thoughts Aspirations lead to efforts that in turn yield success joy sustenance. Our mind then begins to throw sparks of excitement, our heart glows and spreads fragrance in our town akin to beautiful flowers in a well-tended garden.

How should our desires be? The Upanishad says our desires must be multi-faceted, that shows our heart is strong, courageous and large. Our aims must reflect our intellect and reason to be forgiving, accepting, and all-compassing.

The Upanishad goes on to say, infinite may be your desires, all shall be addressed, nay fulfilled.

An analogy of the six tastes and six seasons is given, for us to be able to enjoy and excel in each. *It also means that if one does not like a taste or a season, sure enough, that which one desires or likes is also available and soon coming.*

Six tastes are calming sweet, funny sour, biting pungent, angry bitter, curing astringent, and necessary salty.

Six seasons are life-giving summer, life-nourishing rainy, life-respecting autumn, life-growing winter, life-strengthening extreme cold, and life-exciting spring.

क्रियाशक्तिः पीठम् । कुण्डलिनी ज्ञानशक्तिः गृहम् ।
इच्छाशक्तिर्महात्रिपुरसुन्दरी । ज्ञाता होता ज्ञानमग्निः ज्ञेयꣳ हविः ।
ज्ञातृज्ञानज्ञेयानामभेदभावनꣳ श्रीचक्रपूजनम् ॥ ८ ॥

kriyā-śakti× pīṭham | kuṇḍalinī jñāna-śakti× gṛham | icchā-
śaktirmahātripurasundarī | jñātā hotā jñānamagniḥ jñeya×
haviḥ | jñātṛ-jñāna-jñeyānāmabhedabhāvana× śrī-cakra-
pūjanam ||

क्रियाशक्तिः पीठम् । कुण्डलिनी ज्ञानशक्तिः गृहम् । इच्छाशक्तिः
महात्रिपुरसुन्दरी । ज्ञाता होता ज्ञानम् अग्निः ज्ञेयम् हविः । ज्ञातृज्ञानज्ञेयानाम्
अभेदभावनम् श्रीचक्रपूजनम् ॥

क्रिया-शक्तिः $^{m1/1}$ action-propelling energy पीठम् $^{n2/1}$
foundation (is) । कुण्डलिनी $^{f1/1}$ Kundalini energy ज्ञान-शक्तिः
$^{m1/1}$ wisdom-infused energy गृहम् $^{n2/1}$ home (brings one) ।
इच्छा-शक्तिः $^{m1/1}$ intent (positive) महात्रिपुरसुन्दरी $^{f1/1}$ the
beautiful majestic goddess ruling over the 3 worlds (leads
to) । ज्ञाता $^{m1/1}$ knower होता $^{m1/1}$ worshipper ज्ञानम् $^{n1/1}$
knowledge अग्निः $^{m1/1}$ fire-ritual ज्ञेयम् $^{n1/1}$ known हविः $^{n1/1}$
oblation । ज्ञातृ-ज्ञान-ज्ञेयानाम् $^{n6/3}$ of the knower knowledge
and object known अभेद-भावनम् $^{n1/1}$ undifferentiated
emotion श्री-चक्र-पूजनम् $^{n1/1}$ Sri Chakra Worship (is) ॥

हविः from हविस् ।

This verse is the defining verse of Bhavana Upanishad. It is
the crux of the Sri Yantra. Beautifully it states that a sense of
devotion, gratefulness, and offering one's love is true
worship.

Meaning of Sri Chakra Worship

8. To begin with, a foundation is built by doing a strong powerful action. Then the inner wisdom in the form of the ultra powerful Kundalini Shakti awakens to guide us further on the path. And then one's intent becomes purified and leads one to the Beautiful Blissful Divine Goddess, we all yearn for, an icon of freedom and complete enlightenment.

Knower Knowledge Known. Insight on this triad is given with an analogy.

Knower = the being or soul that directs the body-mind.
Knowledge = an understanding and clarity in the mind.
Known = the object of knowledge. It can be a physical thing or person. Or it can be a theoretical idea or principle.

The analogy makes use of the daily practice of havan (fire ritual) in Indian households, so that the reader can relate to it and grasp it easily.

The analogy says that consider
- Knower to be the one who is performing the fire ritual, with precise control and exuding joy
- Knowledge to be the divine act of performance
- Known to be the ghee (clarified butter) used as the oblation

After all, only someone who has experienced the bountiful grace of a fire-ritual and reaped its immense rewards can consider it as a worshipful, reverential, divine act.

For anyone unfamiliar, it will not evoke relevant emotion.

The Upanishad further says that the sublime understanding in the back of the mind that this triad:

- knower knowledge known are simply one,
- or simply aspects of the same,
- or modes of expression of the one undivided universal consciousness

to develop such an understanding is the actual aim of the Sri Chakra. To unify one's heart, mind and soul with the body is the actual purpose of the Sri Yantra.

When one constructs the Sri Yantra with reverence, and looks upon its constructed form with awe, that is when the benevolence of the Sri Yantra manifests.

This whole process is what is called Sri Chakra worship.

This is what delivers success and bestows grace. This is the harbinger of peace, prosperity and exponential growth in one's city and one's surroundings wherever we go.

Sri Yantra Complete

Sri Yantra Complete with Inscriptions

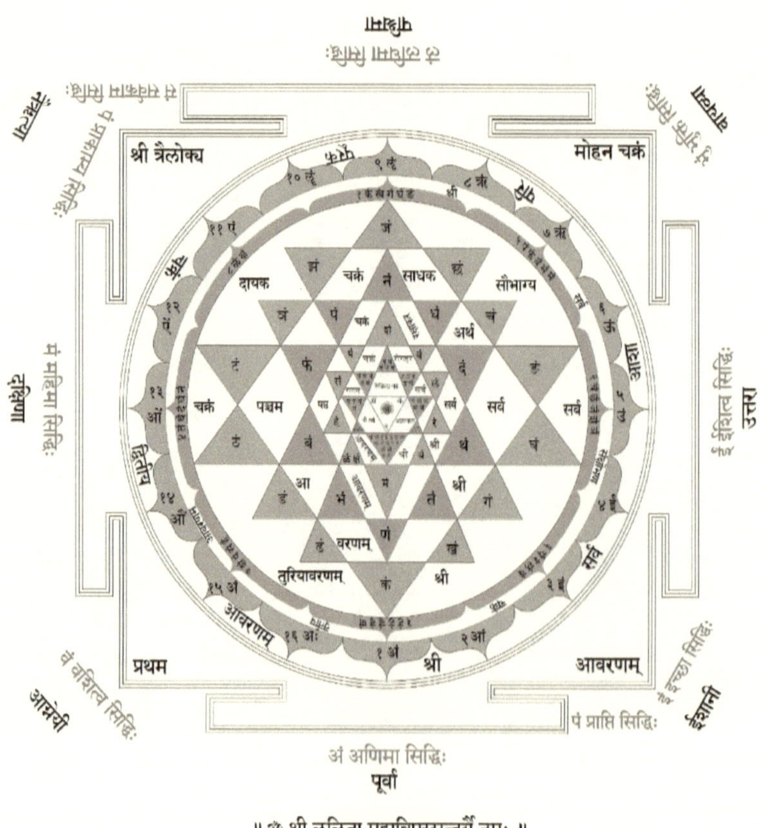

॥ ॐ श्री ललिता महात्रिपुरसुन्दर्यै नमः ॥

श्री यन्त्रम्

Notice that the Bindu aligns perfectly with the Heart Center of Mother Divine.

Avaranas - the Nine Enclosures

And their Sanskrit Alphabet Letters, i.e., Seed Sounds.

नव आवरण A discussion and drawing of the Nine Enclosures is given herein.

1. त्रैलोक्यमोहन चक्रं that which attracts, impresses and infatuates all the three worlds
2. सर्व आशापरिपूरक चक्रं that which fulfills desires and needs of all
3. सर्व संक्षोभण चक्रं that which attracts, impresses and infatuates all the three worlds
4. सर्व सौभाग्यदायक चक्रं that which proves to be fortunate for all
5. सर्वार्थसाधक चक्रं that which provides for and nourishes all
6. सर्व रक्षाकर चक्रं that which protects and guards all
7. सर्व रोगहर चक्रं that which banishes illness and grief from all
8. सर्व सिद्धिप्रद चक्रं that which enhances the talents of each and blossoms everyone
9. सर्व आनन्दमय चक्रं that which infuses bliss, the pure undiluted joy in everyone

Directions in a Sri Yantra

In the Sri Yantra, we travel **anticlockwise** since East is depicted below.

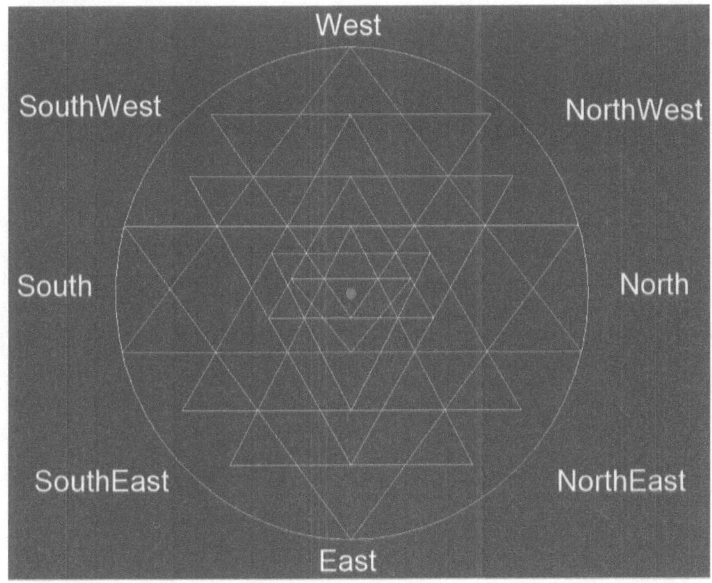

The Sequence is:
i. East ii. NorthEast iii. North iv. NorthWest
v. West vi. SouthWest vii. South viii. SouthEast

1st Enclosure Prathamā Āvaraṇa – Four Square Gates

भूपुर Bhūpura श्री त्रैलोक्यमोहन चक्रं प्रथमावरणम्

नियति सहिताः शृङ्गाः आदयो नव-रसाः अणिमा आदयः । काम-क्रोध-लोभ-मोह-मद-मात्सर्य-पुण्य-पापमय्यी ब्राह्मि आदि अष्ट शक्तयः । आधर-नवकं मुद्रा-शक्तयः ॥ ९ ॥

niyati sahitāḥ śarṅgāḥ ādayo nava-rasāḥ aṇimā ādayaḥ |
kāma-krodha-lobha-moha-mada-mātsarya-puṇya-pāpamayyī
brāhmi ādi aṣṭa śaktayaḥ | ādhara-navakaṃ mudrā-śaktayaḥ

|| 9 ||

Linked to mankind's hope and destiny and evolution,
- the 9 emotions of the heart, Perfection etc., are named as Anima etc., respectively. Anima is the term for miniscule, tiny, atomic. These 9 constitute the siddhis that humans aspire for.

Desire, Anger, Greed, Infatuation, Pride, Envy, Meritorious deeds, and Improper deeds due to weakness; constitute the 8 responses, named Brahmi etc.
- theses 8 responses of man are governed by divinities named Brahmi etc.

The 9 apertures in a human body point towards the proper posture.
- Proper posture is a must so that the 9 openings in the body can function normally and give man appropriate strength and power in day to day activity.

1st avarana प्रथम-आवरणम् = श्री त्रैलोक्य मोहन चक्रं

We start from East bottom and move clockwise. Consists of 10 siddhis.

E   01 अं अणिमा सिद्ध्यै नमः ॥

S   02 मं महिमा सिद्ध्यै नमः ॥

W   03 लं लघिमा सिद्ध्यै नमः ॥

N   04 ई ईशित्व सिद्ध्यै नमः ॥

SE 05 वं वशित्व सिद्ध्यै नमः ॥

SW 06 पं प्राकाम्य सिद्ध्यै नमः ॥

NW 07 भुं भुक्ति सिद्ध्यै नमः ॥

NE 08 इं इच्छा सिद्ध्यै नमः ॥

NE to SW diagonal has two devatas each.
NE 09 पं प्राप्ति सिद्ध्यै नमः ॥

SW 10 सं सर्वकाम सिद्ध्यै नमः ॥

Move Clockwise, starting from अं bottom tip (East). Cover the 4 Cardinal Directions E S W N.

Now move Clockwise, starting from वं bottom left tip (South East). Ordinal Directions SE SW NW NE.

1. East अं अणिमासिद्धिः 2. South मं महिमासिद्धिः 3. West लं लघिमासिद्धिः 4. North ई ईशित्वसिद्धिः

5. SouthEast वं वशित्वसिद्धिः 6. SouthWest पं प्राकाम्यसिद्धिः 7. NorthWest भुं भुक्तिसिद्धिः 8. NorthEast इं इच्छासिद्धिः

<u>NE to SW diagonal has two divinities each.</u>
9. NE पं प्राप्तिसिद्धिः 10. SW सं सर्वकामसिद्धिः

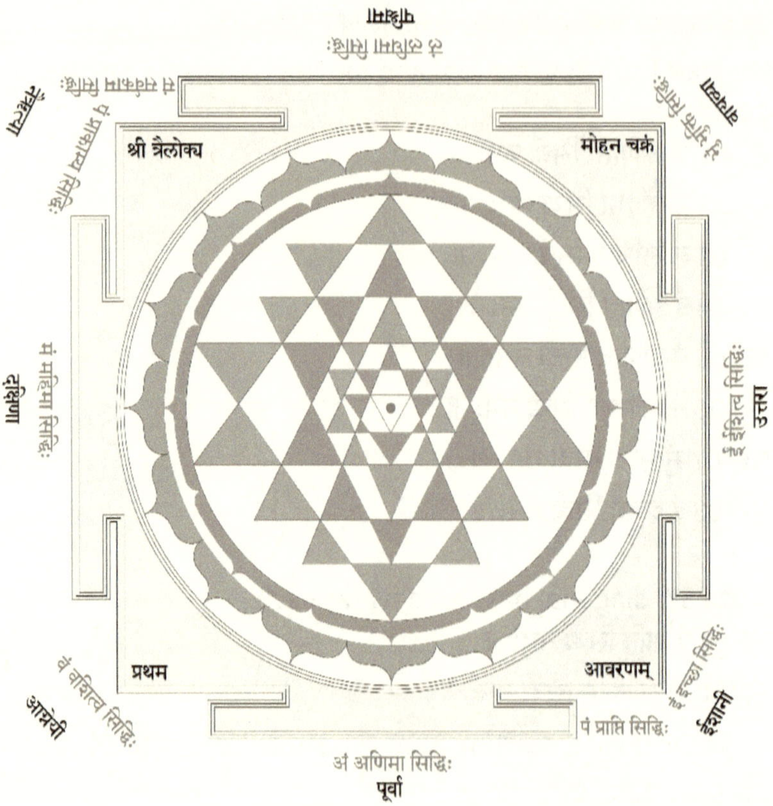

पश्चिमा
लं लघिमा सिद्धिः
नैऋत्या
सं सर्वकाम सिद्धिः
पं प्राकाम्य सिद्धिः
वायव्या
भुं भुक्ति सिद्धिः
श्री त्रैलोक्य
मोहन चक्र
दक्षिणा
मं महिमा सिद्धिः
ईं ईशित्व सिद्धिः
उत्तरा
प्रथम
आवरणम्
वं वशित्व सिद्धिः
आग्नेयी
इं इच्छा सिद्धिः
ईशानी
पं प्राप्ति सिद्धिः
अं अणिमा सिद्धिः
पूर्वा

2nd Enclosure Dvitīyā Āvaraṇa – Sixteen Flower Petals

षोडशदल पद्म Ṣoḍaśadala Padma श्री सर्वाशा परिपूरक चक्रं द्वितीयावरणम्

पृथिवी-अप-तेजः-वायु-आकाशा-श्रोत्र-त्वक्-चक्षुः-जिह्वा-घ्राण-वाक्-पाणि-पाद्-पायु-उपस्थ-मनोविकाराः कामाकर्षिणी आदि षोडश शक्तयः ॥ १० ॥
pṛthivī-apa-tejaḥ-vāyu-ākāśa-śrotra-tvak-cakṣuḥ-jihvā-ghrāṇa-vāk-pāṇi-pāda-pāyu-upastha-manovikārāḥ kāmākarṣiṇī ādi ṣoḍaśa śaktayaḥ ॥ 10 ॥

The elements Earth, Water, Fire, Air, Space; their sense attributes in reverse order - ears, skin, eyes, tongue, nose; and the organs of action Tongue, Hands, Feet, Anus, Penis; and the modifications of the mind; these are the sixteen divinities named Kamakarshini etc., stationed at this perimeter.

dvitīyāvaraṇa द्वितीयावरण = द्वितीय-आवरणम् sarvāśā paripūraka cakra श्री सर्व आशा परिपूरक चक्रं
Each petal has a vowel and the name of a goddess.
1. अं कामाकर्षिणी नित्यकलादेवी Kāmākarṣiṇī nityakalādevī
2. आं बुद्ध्यकर्षिणी नित्यकलादेवी Buddhyakarṣiṇī nityakalādevī
3. इं अहंकाराकर्षिणी नित्यकलादेवी Ahaṁkārākarṣiṇī nityakalādevī
4. ई शब्दाकर्षिणी नित्यकलादेवी Śabdākarṣiṇī nityakalādevī
5. उं स्पर्शाकर्षिणी नित्यकलादेवी Sparśākarṣiṇī nityakalādevī
6. ऊं रूपाकर्षिणी नित्यकलादेवी Rūpākarṣiṇī nityakalādevī
7. ऋं रसाकर्षिणी नित्यकलादेवी Rasākarṣiṇī nityakalādevī

8. ऋं गन्धाकर्षिणी नित्यकलादेवी Gandhākarṣiṇī nityakalādevī

9. ऌं चित्ताकर्षिणी नित्यकलादेवी Cittākarṣiṇī nityakalādevī

10. ॡं धैर्याकर्षिणी नित्यकलादेवी Dhairyākarṣiṇī nityakalādevī

11. एं स्मृत्याकर्षिणी नित्यकलादेवी Smṛtyāākarṣiṇī nityakalādevī

12. ऐं नामाकर्षिणी नित्यकलादेवी Nāmākarṣiṇī nityakalādevī

13. ओं बीजाकर्षिणी नित्यकलादेवी Bījākarṣiṇī nityakalādevī

14. औं आत्माकर्षिणी नित्यकलादेवी Ātmākarṣiṇī nityakalādevī

15. अं अमृताकर्षिणी नित्यकलादेवी Amṛtākarṣiṇī nityakalādevī

16. अः शरीराकर्षिणी नित्यकलादेवी Śarīrākarṣiṇī nityakalādevī

अं कामाकर्षिण्यै नमः ॥ आं बुध्याकर्षिण्यै नमः ॥ इं अहंकाराकर्षिण्यै नमः ॥ ईं शब्दाकर्षिण्यै नमः ॥ उं स्पर्शाकर्षिण्यै नमः ॥ ऊं रूपाकर्षिण्यै नमः ॥ ऋं रसाकर्षिण्यै नमः ॥ ऋं गन्धाकर्षिण्यै नमः ॥ ऌं चित्ताकर्षिण्यै नमः ॥ ॡं धैर्याकर्षिण्यै नमः ॥ एं स्मृत्याकर्षिण्यै नमः ॥ ऐं नामाकर्षिण्यै नमः ॥ ओं बीजाकर्षिण्यै नमः ॥ औं आत्माकर्षिण्यै नमः ॥ अं अमृताकर्षिण्यै नमः ॥ अः शरीराकर्षिण्यै नमः ॥

Move AntiClockwise, starting from अं bottom tip (East).
Cover Sixteen Petals.
अं = nazalised vowel
आं इं ईं उं ऊं ऋं ऋं ऌं ॡं एं ऐं ओं औं = in sequence the vowels of the Sanskrit Alphabet
Followed by the ayogavahas अं अः = till the end of the sixteen petals of the 2nd enclosure.

3rd Enclosure Tṛtīyā Āvaraṇa – Eight Flower Petals

3rd Enclosure –Eight Petalled Lotus = अष्टदल पद्म Aṣṭadala Padma श्री सर्व सौभाग्यदायक चक्रं तृतीयावरणम्

वचन-आदान-गमन-विसर्ग-आनन्द-हान-उपादान-उपेक्षा-बुद्धयः अन्-अङ्ग-कुसुमा आदि अष्टौ शक्तयः ॥ ११ ॥

vacana-ādāna-gamana-visarga-ānanda-hāna-upādāna-upekṣā-buddhayaḥ an-aṅga-kusumā ādi aṣṭau śaktayaḥ ‖ 11 ‖

Soulful Speech, Acceptance of peoples and situations, Exploring far and beyond, Shedding unwanted stuff, Experiencing bliss, Sacrificing, Acquiring Wisdom, and Detachment, are the qualities of a mature and evolved intellect. These constitute the eight bodiless divinities named Kusuma etc.

tṛtīyāvaraṇam तृतीयावरणम् = तृतीय-आवरणम् sarva saṃkṣobhaṇa cakra श्री सर्व संक्षोभण चक्रं

8 petals - Clockwise starting from top petal (west) going alternative petals
each petal has a consonant group (starting letter) and the name of a goddess
Move Clockwise, starting from कं top tip (West). Cover the 4 Cardinal Directions W N E S.
1. West कं खं गं घं ङं अनङ्ग कुसुमा देवी anaṅga kusumā devī
2. North चं छं जं झं ञं अनङ्ग मेखला देवी anaṅga mekhalā devī
3. East टं ठं डं ढं णं अनङ्ग मदना देवी anaṅga madanā devī
4. South तं थं दं धं नं अनंग मदनातुरा देवी anaṅga madanāturā devī

Now move Clockwise, starting from पं top right tip (North West). Ordinal Directions NW NE SE SW.

5. NorthWest पं फं बं भं मं अनङ्ग रेखा देवी anaṅga rekhā devī

6. NorthEast यं रं लं वं अनङ्ग वेगिनी देवी anaṅga veginī devī

7. SouthEast शं षं सं हं अनङ्ग अङ्कुशा देवी anaṅga aṅkuśā devī

8. SouthWest ळं क्षं अनङ्ग मालिनी देवी anaṅga mālinī devī

Move Clockwise, starting from कं top tip (West). Cover the 4 Cardinal Directions W N E S.

1. West कं खं गं घं ङं 2. North चं छं जं झं ञं 3. East टं ठं डं ढं णं 4. South तं थं दं धं नं

Now move Clockwise, starting from पं top right tip (North West). Ordinal Directions NW NE SE SW.

5. NorthWest पं फं बं भं मं 6. NorthEast यं रं लं वं 7. SouthEast शं षं सं हं 8. SouthWest ळं क्षं

4th Enclosure Turiyā Āvaraṇa – Fourteen Triangles

चतुर्दशार Caturdaśāra श्री सर्व सौभाग्यदायक चक्रं तुरियावरणम्
(In spiritual texts, the **fourth** state is called the **Turiya**).

अलम्बुषा कुहूः विश्वोदरा वारणा हस्तिजिह्वा यशोवती पयस्विनी गान्धारी पूषा
शङ्खिनी सरस्वती इडा पिङ्गला सुषुम्ना चेति चतुर्दशः नाड्यः ॥ १२ ॥ सर्व-
संक्षोभिणी आदि चतुर्दशारगाः देवताः ॥ १३ ॥
alambuṣā kuhūḥ viśvodarā vāraṇā hastijihvā yaśovatī
payasvinī gāndhārī pūṣā śaṅkhinī sarasvatī iḍā piṅgalā
suṣumnā ceti caturdaśaḥ nāḍyaḥ ॥ 12 ॥ sarva-saṃkṣobhiṇī

ādi caturdaśāragāḥ devatāḥ ॥ 13 ॥

Alambusha, Kuhu, Vishvodara, Hastijihva, Yashovati,
Payasvini, Gandhari, Pusha, Sankhini, Saraswati, ida,
Pingala, and Sushumna are the fourteen subtle channels
nadi. Their corresponding divinities named
Sarvasankshobhini, etc. rule the fourteen triangles.

turiyāvaraṇa (fourth enclosure) तुरियावरणम् sarva-saubhāgya-

dāyaka cakra श्री सर्व सौभाग्य-दायक चक्रं

fourteen outer triangles - we go anticlockwise this time
beginning from East (bottom)

with consonants in each triangle beginning with क.

कं सर्वसंक्षोभिणी शक्ति East 1. Sarvasaṃkṣobhiṇī śakti

खं सर्वविद्रविणी शक्ति 2.Sarvavidraviṇī śakti

गं सर्वाकर्षिणि शक्ति 3. Sarvākarṣiṇi

घं सर्वाह्लादिनी शक्ति 4. Sarvāhlādinī

ङं सर्वसंमोहिनी शक्ति 5. Sarvasaṁmohinī

चं सर्वस्तंभिनी शक्ति 6. Sarvastaṁbhinī

छं सर्वजृंभिणी शक्ति 7. Sarvajṛṁbhiṇī

जं सर्ववशङ्करी शक्ति 8. Sarvavaśaṅkarī

झं सर्वरञ्जनी शक्ति 9. Sarvarañjanī

ञं सर्वोन्मादिनी शक्ति 10. Sarvonmādinī

टं सर्वार्थसाधिनी शक्ति 11. Sarvārthasādhinī

ठं सर्वसंपत्तिपूरणी शक्ति 12. Sarvasaṁpattipūraṇī

डं सर्वमन्त्रमयी शक्ति 13. Sarvamantramayī

ढं सर्वद्वन्द्वक्षयङ्करी शक्ति 14. Sarvadvandvakṣayaṅkarī śakti

कं सर्व संक्षोभिण्यै नमः ॥ खं सर्व विद्राविण्यै नमः ॥ गं सर्व आकर्षिण्यै नमः ॥

घं सर्वा ह्लादिन्यै नमः ॥ ङं सर्व संमोहिन्यै नमः ॥ चं सर्व स्तंभिन्यै नमः ॥ छं

सर्व जृंभिन्यै नमः ॥ जं सर्व वशंकयैं नमः ॥ झं सर्व रंजन्यै नमः ॥ ञं

सर्वोन्मादिन्यै नमः ॥ टं सर्वाथ साधिन्यै नमः ॥ ठं सर्व संपत्ति पूरिण्यै नमः ॥

डं सर्व मंत्रमय्यै नमः ॥ ढं सर्व द्वैद्वक्षयं कयैं नमः ॥

Move AntiClockwise, starting from कं bottom tip (East).
Cover Fourteen Triangles.
कं = nazalised consonant begins, the Sanskrit Alphabet in continuation from 3rd enclosure
खं गं घं ङं चं छं जं झं ञं टं ठं डं ढं = till the end of the fourteen triangles of the 4th enclosure.

यः एवं वेद , आत्मना आत्मानं एव संविशति the one who so understands, by the Self into the Self alone he merges.

5th Enclosure Pañcamā Āvaraṇa – Ten Outer Triangles

बहिर्दशार BahirDaśāra श्री सर्वार्थसाधक चक्रं पञ्चमावरणम्

प्राण-अपान-व्यान-उदान-समान-नाग-कूर्म-कृकर-देवदत्त-धनञ्जयाः इति दश वायवः । सर्व-सिद्धिप्रदा आदि बहिर्दशारगाः देवताः ॥ १४ ॥

prāṇa-apāna-vyāna-udāna-samāna-nāga-kūrma-kṛkara-devadatta-dhanañjayāḥ iti daśa vāyavaḥ | sarva-siddhipradā ādi bahirdaśāragāḥ devatāḥ ॥ 14 ॥

The vital airs named
- Prana, Apana, Vyana, Udana, Samana;
- Naga, Kurma, Krikara, Devadutta, Dhananjaya

constitute the divinites guarding the ten outer triangles.

fifth āvaraṇa pañcamāvaraṇa पञ्चमावरणम्

Sarvārthasādhakacakra श्री सर्व अर्थ-साधक चक्रं

Ten triangles - we go anticlockwise this time beginning from East (bottom).

With consonants in each triangle in continuation from above.

णं सर्वसिद्धिप्रदा देवी East 1. Sarvasiddhipradā devī

तं सर्वसंपत्प्रदा देवी 2. Sarvasaṃpatpradā devī

थं सर्वप्रियङ्करी देवी 3. Sarvapriyaṅkarī devī

दं सर्वमङ्गलकारिणी देवी 4. Sarvamaṅgalakāriṇī devī

धं सर्वकामप्रदा देवी 5. Sarvakāmapradā devī

नं सर्वदुःखविमोचिनी देवी 6. Sarvaduḥkhavimocinī devī

पं सर्वमृत्युप्रशमनी देवी 7. Sarvamṛtyupraśamanī devī

फं सर्विघ्ननिवारिणी देवी 8. sarvighnanivāriṇī devī

बं सर्वाङ्गसुन्दरी देवी 9. Sarvāṅgasundarī devī

भं सर्वसौभाग्यदायिनी देवी 10. Sarvasaubhāgyadāyinī devī

णं सर्वसिद्धि प्रदायै नमः ॥

तं सर्व संपत् प्रदायै नमः ॥ थं सर्व प्रियंकर्यै नमः ॥ दं सर्व मंगल कारिण्यै नमः ॥

धं सर्व कामप्रदायै नमः ॥

नं सर्व दुःख विमोचिन्यै नमः ॥

पं सर्व मृत्यु प्रशामन्यै नमः ॥ फं सर्व विघ्न निवारिण्यै नमः ॥ बं सर्वांग सुंदर्यै

नमः ॥ भं सर्व सौभाग्य दायियन्यै नमः ॥

Move AntiClockwise, starting from णं bottom tip (East).

Cover Ten Triangles.

Notes:

णं = nazalised consonant in continuation from 4th enclosure

तं थं दं धं नं पं फं बं भं = till the end of the ten triangles of the 5th enclosure.

6th Enclosure Ṣaṣṭhā Āvaraṇa – Ten Inner Triangles

अन्तर्दशार AntarDaśāra श्री सर्वं रक्षाकर चक्रं षष्ठावरणम्

एतद् वायु-दशकः संसर्ग-उपाधि-भेधेन रेचक-पाचक-शोषक-दाहक-प्लावकाः अमृतम् इति प्राण-मुख्यत्वेन पञ्चधा जठर-अग्निः भवति । क्षारकः उद्घारकः क्षोभकः मोहकः जृम्भकः इति नाग-प्राधान्येन पञ्चविधोऽस्ति । तेन मनुष्याणां देहानां भक्ष्य-भोज्य-चोष्य-लेह्य-पेयात्मकं पञ्चविधम्-अन्नं पाचयन्ति । एता दश वह्निकलाः सर्वज्ञाद्याः अन्तर्दशारगाः देवताः ॥ १५ ॥

etad vāyu-daśaka saṃsargopādhibhedhena recaka-pacaka-
śoṣaka-dāhaka-plāvakāḥamṛtam iti prāṇamukhyatvena
pañcadhā jaṭhara-agniḥ bhavati | kṣārakaḥ udgārakaḥ
kṣobhakaḥ mohakaḥ jṛmbhakaḥ iti nāga-prādhānyena
pañcavidho'sti | tena manuṣyāṇāṃ mohako dāhako bhakṣya-
bhojya-coṣya-lehya-peyātmakaṃ pañcavidham-annaṃ
pācayanti | etā daśa vahnikalāḥ sarvajñādyāḥ antardaśāragā
devatāḥ || 15 ||

As per the prevailing situation and demand, the same ten-
fold Prana:
functions as the five-fold **main** Prana as
- The Remover of toxins
- The Digester of good emotions, thoughts, and food
- The Smoother of slushy, nagging and sticky emotions
- The Vanquisher of painful memories
- The Submerger of traumatic thoughts, to stoke the digestive fires in the stomach and abdomen,

and led by the upaPrana named Naga functions as the five-fold **secondary** Prana as

- The Secreter
- The Ejector
- The Churner
- The Sweller
- The Yawner

These constitute the divinites guarding the ten inner triangles.

sixth āvaraṇa (ṣaṣṭhāvaraṇa) षष्ठावरणम् Sarvarakṣākaracakra श्री सर्व रक्षा-कर चक्रं

Ten triangles - we go anticlockwise this time beginning from East (bottom)

with consonants in each triangle in continuation from above.

मं सर्वज्ञादेवी East 1. Sarvajñādevī

यं सर्वशक्तिप्रदादेवी 2. Sarvaśaktidevī

रं सर्वैश्वर्यप्रदादेवी 3. Sarvaiśvaryapradādevī

लं सर्वज्ञानमयीदेवी 4. Sarvajñānamayīdevī

वं सर्वव्याधिविनाशिनीदेवी 5. Sarvavyādhivināśinīdevī

शं सर्वाधारादेवी 6. Sarvādhārādevī

षं सर्वपापहरादेवी 7. Sarvapāpaharādevī

सं सर्वानन्दमयीदेवी 8. Sarvānandamayīdevī

हं सर्वरक्षास्वरूपिणीदेवी 9. Sarvarakṣāsvarūpiṇīdevī

ळं क्षं सर्वेप्सितफलप्रदादेवी 10. Sarvepsitaphalapradādevī

मं सर्वज्ञायै नमः ॥ यं सर्व शक्तै नमः ॥ रं सर्वैश्वर्य प्रदायै नमः ॥ लं ज्ञानमय्यै नमः ॥ वं सर्व व्याधि विनाशिन्यै नमः ॥

शं सर्वाधार स्वरूपायै नमः ॥ षं सर्व पापहरायै नमः ॥ सं सर्वानंदमयू नमः ॥

हं सर्व रक्षारूपीणीयै नमः ॥

ळं क्षं सर्वेप्सित फलप्रदायै नमः ॥

Move AntiClockwise, starting from मं bottom tip (East). Cover Ten Triangles.

Notes:

मं = nazalised consonant in continuation from 5th enclosure

यं लं रं वं शं षं सं हं = till the end of the standard Sanskrit Alphabet

ळं क्षं = additional letters of the Vedic Sanskrit Alphabet

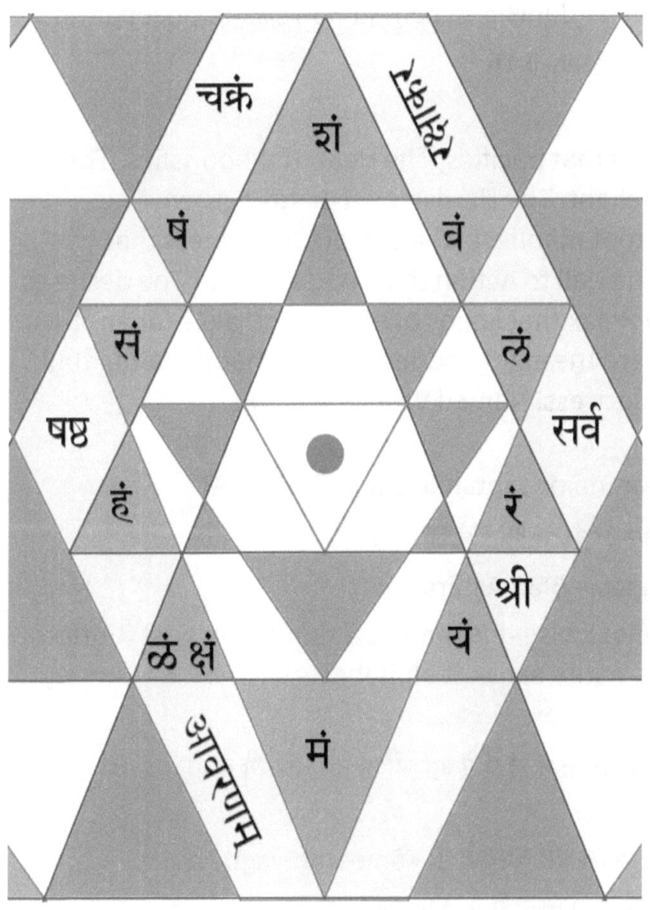

7th Enclosure Saptamā Āvaraṇa – Eight Triangles

अष्टार Aṣṭāra श्री सर्व रोगहर चक्रं सप्तमावरणम्

शीत-उष्ण-सुख-दुःख-इच्छाः सत्त्व-रजस्-तमोगुणाः वशिनी आदि शक्तयः अष्टौ ॥ १६ ॥

śīta-uṣṇa-sukha-duḥkha-icchāḥ sattva-rajas-tamoguṇāḥ vaśinī ādi śaktayaḥ aṣṭau ॥ 16 ॥

The Coolness that pacifies, The Heat that nourishes, The Joys that delight, The Hardships that strengthen, The Intentions that manifest; The Sincere Awareness that protects, The Call to Action that supports, and The desire to Let Go and Relax that keeps one fresh and alive for another day; these are the eight goddesses circumambulating this wall of the fortress. Named Vashini etc.

seventh āvaraṇa or saptamāvaraṇa सप्तमावरणम्

sarvarogaharacakra श्री सर्व रोग-हर चक्रं

eight triangles – अष्टार Aṣṭāra

we go anticlockwise this time beginning from East (bottom) to write the entire sanskrit alphabet

अं आं इं ईं उं ऊं ऋं ॠं ऌं ॡं एं ऐं ओं औं अं अः वशिनी वाग्देवी East 1. Vaśinī vāgdevī

कं खं गं घं ङं कामेश्वरी वाग्देवी 2. Kāmeśvarī vāgdevī

चं छं जं झं ञं मोदिनी वाग्देवी 3. Modinī vāgdevī

टं ठं डं ढं णं विमला वाग्देवी 4. Vimalā vāgdevī

तं थं दं धं नं अरुणा वाग्देवी 5. Aruṇā vāgdevī

पं फं बं भं मं जैनि वाग्देवी 6. Jaini vāgdevī

यं रं लं वं सर्वेश्वरी वाग्देवी 7. Sarveśvarī vāgdevī

शं षं सं हं ळं क्षं कौलिनी वाग्देवी 8. Kaulinī vāgdevī

1 East अं आं इं ईं उं ऊं ऋं ॠं लृं ॡं एं ऐं ओं औं अं अः ब्ल्रूं वशिनी वाग्देवतायै नमः ॥

2 कं खं गं घं ङं क्ल्हीं कामेश्वरी वाग्देवतायै नमः ॥ 3 चं छं जं झं ञं न्ह्रीं मोदिनी वाग्देवतायै नमः ॥ 4 टं ठं डं ढं णं य्ल्रूं विमला वाग्देवतायै नमः ॥ 5 तं थं दं धं नं ज्म्रीं अरुणा वाग्देवतायै नमः ॥ 6 पं फं बं भं मं हूस्ल्व्यूं जयिनी वाग्देवतायै नमः ॥ 7 यं रं लं वं इन्रयूं सर्वेश्वरी वाग्देवतायै नमः ॥ 8 शं षं सं हं ळं क्षं क्ष्म्रीं कौलिनी वाग्देवतायै नमः ॥

Move AntiClockwise, starting from अच् bottom tip (East).

Cover Eight Triangles. Called अष्टार Aṣṭāra.

Notes: Here we write the complete Sanskrit Alphabet, representing all the Speech Goddesses.

From अं to क्षं

8th Enclosure Aṣṭamā Āvaraṇa – Innermost Triangle

8th Enclosure – Innermost Triangle = त्रिकोण Trikoṇa श्री सर्व सिद्धिप्रद चक्रं अष्टमावरणम्

शाब्द-स्पर्श-रूप-रस-गन्धाः पञ्च-तन्मात्राः पञ्च-पुष्पबाणाः । मनः इक्षु-धनुः । रागः पाशः । द्वेषः अङ्कुशः ॥ १७ ॥ śabda-sparśa-rūpa-rasa-gandhāḥ pañca-tanmātrāḥ pañca-puṣpabāṇāḥ l manaḥ ikṣu-dhanuḥ l rāgaḥ pāśaḥ l dveṣaḥ aṅkuśaḥ ॥ 17 ॥

- Sound, Touch, Form, Taste, Smell are the five direct sensory tolerances, and are called the five alluring arrows.
- The thought producing Mind is the desirous bow ever shooting outwards
- The feeling of Infatuation is that which initially entangles and ultimately strangles
- The feeling of Aversion is that which hobbles and restricts one's own evolution.

अव्यक्त-महत्तत्त्वम्-महत्अहङ्काराः इति कामेश्वरी-वज्रेश्वरी-भगमालिनी अन्तस् त्रिकोण-अग्रगाः देवताः ॥ १८ ॥
avyakta-mahattattvam-mahatahaṅkārāḥ iti kāmeśvarī-vajreśvarī-bhagamālinī antas trikoṇa-agragāḥ devatāḥ ॥ 18 ॥

- The unmanifest primordial nature,
- The individual consciousness, and
- The human ego

are the leading divinities of this innermost triangle, also named Kameshwari, Vajreshwari, Bhagamalini.

Eighth āvaraṇa or aṣṭamāvaraṇam अष्टमावरणं called
Sarvasiddhiprada श्री सर्व सिद्धि-प्रद चक्रं
one downward pointing triangle, white in color
we go clockwise this time beginning from East (bottom)

Tripurāṁbācakreśvarī

East - Triangle Apex Down 1. ऐं
Triangle base left 2. क्लीं
Triangle base right 3. सौः
Move Clockwise, starting from ऐं bottom tip (East).
Notes: Here we write the symbols of Mother Divine

सिद्धिप्रदा चक्रं
क्लीं
सौः
श्री सर्व
ऐं
अष्टमावरणं

9th Enclosure Navamā Āvaraṇa - Bindu

9th Enclosure – Innermost Dot = बिन्दु Bindu श्री सर्वानन्दमय चक्रं नवमावरणम्

निरुपाधिका संविदेव कामेश्वरः । सदानन्दपूर्णा स्वात्मैव परदेवता ललिता । लौहित्यमेतस्य सर्वस्य विमर्शः ॥ १९ ॥

nirupādhikā saṃvideva kāmeśvaraḥ | sadānandapūrṇā svātmaiva paradevatā lalitā | lauhityametasya sarvasya vimarśaḥ || 19 ||

That which cannot be contained in form, that which is one's innermost self, is called Kameshvara.
And continually filled with bliss, verily one's own innermost self , that which cannot be fathomed is called Lalita. During deep meditation, the ruddy rosy hue of the Self is seen.

श्री सर्वानन्दमय चक्रं नवमावरणम्
Ninth āvaraṇa navamāvaraṇa नवमावरणम् -
sarvānandamayacakra श्री सर्व आनन्द-मय चक्रं
Bindu bindusthāna, red color श्रीं
Śrī Mahātripurasundarī (Śiva-śakty-aikya-rūpiṇī)
श्रीललिता महा त्रिपुर सुंदर्यै नमः

Become Still, Silent, Soft, Melted, Absorbed in Divine Union.

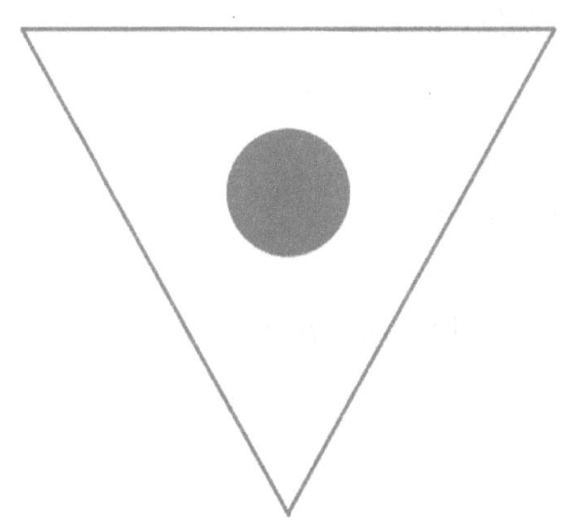

ॐ सर्वानन्दमय चक्रं नवमावरणम्
श्रीं

अनन्यचित्तत्वेन च सिद्धिः ॥ २० ॥

ananyacittatvena ca siddhiḥ ॥

अनन्य-चित्-तत्वेन च सिद्धिः ॥

अनन्य-चित्-तत्वेन [m3/1] by undistracted mind च [0] and सिद्धिः [f1/1] Perfection ॥

Perfection demands sincere one-pointed Focus

20. And only by the sincere laser beam like one pointed mind and integration of all mental faculties can perfection be achieved. Siddhi or Perfection is a fluid grasp of a principle internally and it is then the physical expression of that idea by one's body-mind complex.

Siddhi can loosely be translated as very high talent or skill in something. We see in the world around us, the men and women with exceptional talent in arts, music, sports, administration, engineering or medicine, did not achieve it overnight. They spent long arduous hours in their discipline and sincere practice, and then after a long time their skill got shone on the world stage and was appreciated by all.

After having constructed the Bindu in the innermost triangle of the Sri Yantra, one needs to look at it with ardent devotion and unwavering focus.

The Upanishad is stating the key that can make one's talent shine and get expressed. After all isn't that the reason one got born in a body in the first place?

भावनायाᳵ क्रिया उपचाराः । अहं त्वमस्ति नास्ति
कर्तव्यमकर्तव्यमुपासितव्यमिति विकल्पानामात्मनि विलापनं होमः ।
भावना विषयाणामभेदभावना तर्पणम् ॥ २१ ॥

bhāvanāyāḥ kriyā upacārāḥ | ahaṃ tvam asti nāsti kartavyam
akartavyam upāsitavyam iti vikalpānām ātmani vilāpanaṃ
homaḥ | bhāvanā viṣayāṇām abheda-bhāvanā tarpaṇam ||

भावनायाः क्रियाः उपचाराः । अहम् त्वम् अस्ति नास्ति कर्तव्यम् अकर्तव्यम्
उपासितव्यम् इति विकल्पानाम् आत्मनि विलापनम् होमः । भावना विषयाणाम्
अभेदभावना तर्पणम् ॥

भावनायाः [f6/1] of meditative क्रियाः [f1/3] acts उपचाराः [m1/3]
treatments । अहम् [mfn1/1] I त्वम् [mfn1/1] You अस्ति [लट् iii/1] am
नास्ति [लट् iii/1] am not कर्तव्यम् [0] to do अकर्तव्यम् [0] to do not
उपासितव्यम् [0] to honor इति [0] thus विकल्पानाम् [m6/3] by such
choice of thoughts आत्मनि [m7/1] in innermost self विलापनम् [n1/1]
intense cry होमः [m1/1] Vedic Fire Ritual ।
भावना [f1/1] Emotion विषयाणाम् [m6/3] of matters अभेद-भावना [f1/1]
undifferentiated emotion तर्पणम् [n1/1] offering ||

Meditation Explained

21. Meditation is the prime mover and the direct path to self-realization.

There is no worship without Meditation. What is Worship? Worship is the grateful acknowledgement of the grace in life, the abundance in life, and the happiness one experiences.

By Meditation, life's purpose becomes clear. Life becomes charming as the senses become balanced.

Meditation is that which makes one total. An activity wherein one is fully integrated, absorbed, and at ease.

Dissolution of modifications of the mind is Meditation. Rising above the likes and dislikes, dropping the continuous chatter of logic and reason, and getting established in the Self is Meditation.

Bhavana is a sensory feeling deep inside the Heart. It is a thought beyond the mental gymnastics. Meditation is that same deep emotion, that strikes at the very core of existence. Silent contemplation of the topics and situations and people and physical bonds and limits and coming to peaceful terms with all in the heart is Meditation.

Digesting and assimilating the challenge and praise both is Meditation. It needs a Master. It is a state that can verily be granted by the Guru. It is something that is the fruit of smiling service.

पञ्चदश तिथिरूपेण कालस्य परिणामावलोकनं पञ्चदश नित्याः ॥ २२ ॥
pañcadaśa tithi-rūpeṇa kālasya pariṇāmā avalokanaṃ
pañcadaśa nityāḥ ॥

पञ्चदश तिथिरूपेण कालस्य परिणामावलोकनम् पञ्चदश नित्याः ॥

पञ्चदश ^{mfn1/3} fifteen तिथि-रूपेण ^{n3/1} as per lunar fortnight
कालस्य ^{m6/1} of time परिणाम-अवलोकनम् ^{n2/1} discriminating
upon the results पञ्चदश ^{mfn1/3} fifteen नित्याः ^{adj1/3} eternal ॥

Learn Steadfast Sincerity from the Moon

22. This one-pointed integration of the body-mind is not limited to a single day.

Rather giving the example of the days in a lunar fortnight, how the moon takes 15 days to wax and another 15 days to wane, similarly one is told to be regular in one's practice, regular in maintaining discipline, and avoiding breach of discipline.

The moon is so punctual and regular in its waxing and waning. It never skips. Observe the moon and apply its sincere steadfast behavior. Then we too can attain anything noble and great in life.

एवं मुहूर्तत्रितयं मुहूर्तद्वितयं मुहूर्तमात्रं वा भावनापरो जीवन्मुक्तो भवति ।
स एव शिवयोगी इति गद्यते ॥ २३ ॥

evaṃ muhūrta-tritayaṃ muhūrta-dvitayaṃ muhūrta-mātraṃ
vā bhāvanāparo jīvanmukto bhavati I sa eva śivayogī iti
gadyate II

एवम् मुहूर्तत्रितयम् मुहूर्तद्वितयम् मुहूर्तमात्रम् वा भावनापरः जीवन्मुक्तः भवति ।
सः एव शिवयोगी इति गद्यते ॥

एवम्[0] likewise मुहूर्त-त्रितयम्[n1/1] muhurta-triple मुहूर्त-द्वितयम्[n1/1] muhurta-dual मुहूर्त-मात्रम्[n1/1] muhurta-once only वा[0] or भावना-परः[adj1/1] highest meditation जीवन्-मुक्तः[adj1/1] liberated while alive भवति[लृ iii/1] becomes I सः[m1/1] he एव[0] alone शिव-योगी[m1/1] Shiva Yogi (is) इति[0] thus गद्यते[लृ iii/1] it has been elaborately stated in the Scriptures II

Little Discipline Goes a Long Way

23. If you wish to live a really good life on the planet, maintain your alert focus for the entire day = 3 muhurta. A muhurta is of 8 hours or 1/3rd of a day.

The number 3 is highlighted here again so that one may not forget the math stated earlier.

Now the Upanishad relents and addresses the entire populace.

It says okay, if you wish to perform decently average, then maintain your sincere focus for 2 muhurta, i.e., 2/3rd of a day.

Finally for the weak or the ill or folk who cannot overcome their pleasure seeking senses, or are satisfied with a below par effort, discipline for a duration of 1 muhurta is stated. I.e., 8 hours daily, the standard working hours all over the globe. Even that shall help them overcome their faulty tendencies, albeit in another life, surely after a long long time.

Such a person alone qualifies for Enlightenment. Only someone who incorporates spiritual practices, who strives for sincerity in day-to-day effort, who makes it a point to adhere to self-discipline on a regular basis, qualifies.

Such is a Shiva Yogi, i.e., an Auspicious Being that helps elevate all on the planet, it is said.

कादिमतेन अन्तश्चक्रभावना× प्रतिपादिताः ॥ २४॥

kādimatena antaścakra-bhāvanā× pratipāditāḥ ॥

कादिमतेन अन्तश्चक्रभावनाः प्रतिपादिताः ॥

कृ-आदि-मतेन [n3/1] according to the K-adi philosophy अन्तः-चक्र-भावनाः [f1/3] deepest meditative emotions of the wheel of life प्रति-पादिताः [adj1/3] well expounded ॥

Seed Sounds help in Meditation

24. This is verily the lifestyle for the brave to be adopted.

Adopting this lifestyle is called the K-etc. ideology.

क = K = The starting letter of the consonants of the Sanskrit Alphabet.

The Sanskrit Alphabet has been endowed with divinity and portrayed in the form of divinities governing life, as expressed by the constructed Sri Yantra inscribed with Seed Sounds.

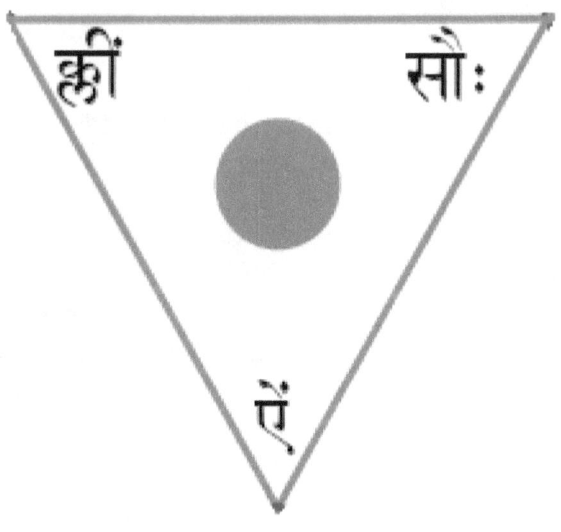

य एवं वेद । सोऽथर्वशिरोऽधीते ॥ २५ ॥
॥ इत्युपनिषत् ॥

ya evaṃ veda | saḥ atharvaśirah adhīte ॥
॥ ityupaniṣat ॥

यः एवम् वेद । सः अथर्वशिरः अधीते ॥
॥ इति उपनिषत् ॥

यः [m1/1] That एवम् [0] likewise वेद [लोट् ii/1] you may know ।
सः [m1/1] he अथर्व-शिरः [m1/1] Atharvaveda Main अधीते [लट् jiii/1] has
well learnt ॥

॥ इति [0] thus here ends उपनिषत् [f1/1] Upanishad ॥

अधीते from Upasarga अधि + Dhatupatha Root 1046. इङ्
अध्ययने 2cA. to learn properly and sincerely

Fountainhead of Atharva Veda Learnt

25. Know this to be the essence of the teaching.

The one who has assimilated this teaching, can be said to be practicing the Main principles of Atharvaveda, the Veda that gives clear, definite, and direct methods and techniques for individuals to live life completely and creatively, and become evolved blissful beings.

This is the teaching that needs a Master. This is the teaching that needs an ardent devotee. This is the teaching that ensures well-being and all round happiness.

Here ends the Upanishad.

There are 4 Veda
The Rigveda expounds the Principles of Creation.
The Samaveda underlines the Harmony in Creation.
The Yajurveda lays down the dictums for Corporations, Institutions and Nations to operate.

The Atharvaveda gives simple techniques for Man to practice a holistic life, how to face challenges and situations, and how to succeed and become prosperous.

Etymology of Upanishad

व्युत्पत्ति
Consider Adi Shankaracharya's derivation of the word 'Upanishad' as given in his bhashyam on the Katha Upanishad.

उप + नि + षद् + क्विप् –> उपनिषद्

The Sanskrit root from Dhatupatha 1c - 854, 6c - 1427 षद्ऌ विशरण–गति–अवसादनेषु has the three meanings, namely

विशरण= wither, गति= attain, अवसादनं = sit.

In the context of wisdom, we can say
- wither away one's stupidity
- attain liberation
- sit with a conviction

The upasarga उप stands for nearness, closeness.
The upasarga नि stands for delving into, intense.
The pratyaya क्विप् makes a noun, and while joining, it vanishes entirely.

Thus the word 'Upanishad' is formed, and it has the meaning of destroying one's ignorance and granting freedom, when we sit devotedly at the feet of the Master.

Latin Transliteration Chart

International Alphabet of Sanskrit Transliteration (I.A.S.T.)

a	आ	i	ई	u	ऊ	r̥	r̥̄	l̥	
अ	आ	इ	ई	उ	ऊ	ऋ	ॠ	ऌ	
						$_{◌ृ}$	$_{◌ॄ}$	$_{◌ॢ}$	
e	ai	o	au	ṃ	m̐	ḥ	Ardha Visarga	oṃ	
ए	ऐ	ओ	औ	◌ं	◌ँ	◌:	◌ᵪ	ॐ	

Consonants shown with vowel 'a= अ' for uttering									
ka	क	ca	च	ṭa	ट	ta	त	pa	प
kha	ख	cha	छ	ṭha	ठ	tha	थ	pha	फ
ga	ग	ja	ज	ḍa	ड	da	द	ba	ब
gha	घ	jha	झ	ḍha	ढ	dha	ध	bha	भ
ṅa	ङ	ña	ञ	ṇa	ण	na	न	ma	म
ya	ra	la	va		ḷa	'			
य	र	ल	व		ळ	S			
					Consonant only				
śa	ṣa	sa	ha		ka	क्अ = क			
श	ष	स	ह		k	क्			

The symbol ꣽ is pronounced as गुं guṃ. It is an ayogavaha अयोगवाह sound seen in Vedic literature due to Sandhi.

Verses for Chanting

॥ अथ भावनोपनिषद् ॥

ॐ भद्रं कर्णेभिः श्रृणुयाम देवाः । भद्रं पश्येम माक्षभिर् यजत्राः । स्थिरैरङ्गैस् तुष्टुवाँ सस्तनूभिः । व्यशेम देवहितं यदायुः ॥ स्वस्ति न इन्द्रो वृद्धश्रवाः । स्वस्ति नः पूषा विश्ववेदाः । स्वस्ति नस्ताक्ष्यों अरिष्टनेमिः । स्वस्ति नो बृहस्पतिर्दधातु ॥ ॐ शान्तिः शान्तिः शान्तिः ॥

ॐ आत्मानम् अखण्डमण्डलाकारम् आवृत्य सकलब्रह्माण्डमण्डलं स्वप्रकाशं ध्यायेत् ।

श्री गुरुः सर्वकारणभूता शक्तिः ॥ १ ॥ तेन नवरन्ध्ररूपो देहः ॥ २ ॥

नवशक्तिरूपꣳ श्रीचक्रम् ॥ ३ ॥

वाराही पितृरूपा । कुरुकुल्ला बलिदेवता माता ॥ ४ ॥

पुरुषार्थाः सागराः ॥ ५ ॥

देहो नवरत्नद्वीपः । त्वगादिसप्तधातुभिः अनेकैः रोमसंयुक्ताः ॥ ६ ॥

सङ्कल्पाः कल्पतरवः । तेजꣳ कल्पकोद्यानम् । रसनया भाव्यमाना मधुराम्लतिक्तकटुकषायलवणरसाः षड् ऋतवः ॥ ७ ॥

क्रियाशक्तिꣳ पीठम् । कुण्डलिनी ज्ञानशक्तिꣳ गृहम् । इच्छाशक्तिर्महात्रिपुरसुन्दरी । ज्ञाता होता ज्ञानमग्निः ज्ञेयꣳ हविः । ज्ञातृज्ञानज्ञेयानामभेदभावनꣳ श्रीचक्रपूजनम् ॥ ८ ॥

नियतिसहिताः शृङ्गारादयो नवरसाः अणिमादयः । कामक्रोधलोभमोहमदमात्सर्यपुण्यपापमय्यी ब्राह्म्याद्यष्टशक्तयः । आधरनवकं मुद्राशक्तयः ॥ ९ ॥

पृथिव्यपतेजोवाय्वाकाश-श्रोत्रत्वक्चक्षुःजिह्वाघ्राण-वाक्पाणिपादपाय्यूपस्थमनोविकाराः कामाकर्षिण्यादि षोडश शक्तयः ॥ १० ॥

वचनादानगमनविसर्गानन्द-हानोपादानोपेक्षाबुद्धयोऽनङ्गकुसुमाद्यष्टौ शक्तयः ॥ ११ ॥

अलम्बुषा कुहूर्विश्वोदरा वारणा हस्तिजिह्वा यशोवती पयस्विनी गान्धारी पूषा
शङ्खिनी सरस्वती इडा पिङ्गला सुषुम्ना चेति चतुर्दश नाड्यः ॥ १२॥

सर्वसंक्षोभिण्यादि चतुर्दशारगा देवताः ॥ १३ ॥

प्राणापानव्यानोदानसमान-नागकूर्मकृकरदेवदत्तधनञ्जया इति दश वायवः ।
सर्वसिद्धिप्रदादि बहिर्दशारगा देवताः ॥ १४ ॥

एतद् वायुदशकः संसर्गोपाधिभेदेन रेचकपाचकशोषकदाहककल्लावका अमृतमिति
प्राणमुख्यत्वेन पञ्चधा जठराग्निर्भवति । क्षारक उद्धारकः क्षोभको मोहको जृम्भक
इति नागप्राधान्येन पञ्चविधोऽस्ति । तेन मनुष्याणां देहानां
भक्ष्यभोज्यचोष्यलेह्यपेयात्मकं पञ्चविधमन्नं पाचयन्ति । एता दश वह्निकलाः
सर्वज्ञाद्या अन्तर्दशारगा देवताः ॥ १५ ॥

शीतोष्णसुखदुःखेच्छाः सत्त्वरजस्तमोगुणा वशिन्यादि शक्तयोऽष्टौ ॥ १६ ॥

शब्दस्पर्शरूपरसगन्धाः पञ्चतन्मात्राः पञ्चपुष्पबाणाः ।
मन इक्षुधनुः । रागः पाशाः । द्वेषोऽङ्कुशः ॥ १७ ॥

अव्यक्तमहत्तत्त्वम्-महदहङ्कारा इति कामेश्वरीवज्रेश्वरीभगमालिन्यन्तस्
त्रिकोणाग्रगा देवताः ॥ १८॥

निरुपाधिका संविदेव कामेश्वरः । सदानन्दपूर्णा स्वात्मैव परदेवता ललिता ।
लौहित्यमेतस्य सर्वस्य विमर्शः ॥ १९॥

अनन्यचित्तत्वेन च सिद्धिः ॥ २०॥

भावनायाः क्रिया उपचाराः । अहं त्वमस्ति नास्ति
कर्तव्यमकर्तव्यमुपासितव्यमिति विकल्पानामात्मनि विलापनं होमः ।
भावना विषयाणामभेदभावना तर्पणम् ॥ २१॥

पञ्चदश तिथिरूपेण कालस्य परिणामावलोकनं पञ्चदश नित्याः ॥ २२॥

एवं मुहूर्तंत्रितयं मुहूर्तंद्वितयं मुहूर्तंमात्रं वा भावनापरो जीवन्मुक्तो भवति ।
स एव शिवयोगी इति गद्यते ॥ २३॥

कादिमतेन अन्तश्चक्रभावनाः प्रतिपादिताः ॥ २४॥

य एवं वेद । सोऽथर्वशिरोऽधीते ॥ २५॥

॥ इत्युपनिषत् ॥

ॐ भद्रं कर्णेभिः श्रृणुयाम देवाः । भद्रं पश्ये माक्षभिर् यजत्राः । स्थिरैरङ्गैस्
तुष्टुवां सस्तनूभिः । व्यशेम देवहितं यदायुः ॥ स्वस्ति न इन्द्रो वृद्धश्रवाः ।
स्वस्ति नः पूषा विश्ववेदाः । स्वस्ति नस्ताक्ष्यों अरिष्टनेमिः । स्वस्ति नो
बृहस्पतिर्दधातु ॥ ॐ शान्तिः शान्तिः शान्तिः ॥

‖ atha bhāvanopaniṣad ‖

oṃ bhadraṃ karṇebhiḥ śṛṇuyāma devāḥ | bhadraṃ paśye
mākṣabhir yajatrāḥ | sthirairaṅgais tuṣṭuvāṃ sastanūbhiḥ |
vyaśema devahitaṃ yadāyuḥ ‖ svasti na indro vṛddhaśravāḥ
| svasti naḥ pūṣā viśvavedāḥ | svasti nastārkṣyo ariṣṭanemiḥ
| svasti no bṛhaspatirdadhātu ‖ oṃ śāntiḥ śāntiḥ śāntiḥ ‖

oṃ ātmānam akhaṇḍa-maṇḍalākāram āvṛtya sakala-
brahmāṇḍa-maṇḍalam svaprakāśam dhyāyet | śrī guruḥ
sarvakāraṇabhūtā śaktiḥ ‖ 1 ‖ tena nava-randhra-rūpo
dehaḥ ‖ 2 ‖ nava-śakti-rūpaⰈ śrī-cakram ‖ 3 ‖ vārāhī
pitṛrūpā | kurukullā balidevatā mātā ‖ 4 ‖ puruṣārthāḥ
sāgarāḥ ‖ 5 ‖ deho nava-ratna-dvīpaḥ | tvak-ādi-sapta-
dhātubhiḥ anekaiḥ saṃyuktāḥ ‖ 6 ‖ saṅkalpāḥ kalpataravaḥ |
tejaⰈ kalpaka-udyānam | rasanayā bhāvyamānā madhuḥ-
āmla-tikta-kaṭu-kaṣāya-lavaṇa-rasāḥ ṣaḍ ṛtavaḥ ‖ 7 ‖ kriyā-
śaktiⰈ pīṭham | kuṇḍalinī jñāna-śaktiⰈ gṛham | icchā-
śaktirmahātripurasundarī | jñātā hotā jñānamagniḥ jñeyaⰈ
haviḥ | jñātṛ-jñāna-jñeyānāmabhedabhāvanaⰈ śrī-cakra-
pūjanam ‖ 8 ‖ niyati sahitāḥ śarṅgāḥ ādayo nava-rasāḥ
aṇimā ādayaḥ | kāma-krodha-lobha-moha-mada-mātsarya-

puṇya-pāpamayyī brāhmi ādi aṣṭa śaktayaḥ | ādhara-navakaṃ mudrā-śaktayaḥ || 9 || pṛthivyapatejovāyvākāśa-śrotratvakcakṣuḥjihvāghrāṇa-vākpāṇipādapāyūpasthamanovikārāḥ kāmākarṣiṇyādi ṣoḍaśa śaktayaḥ || 10 || vacana-ādāna-gamana-visarga-ānanda-hāna-upādāna-upekṣā-buddhayaḥ an-aṅga-kusumā ādi śaktayaḥ aṣṭau || 11 || alambuṣā kuhūḥ viśvodarā vāraṇā hastijihvā yaśovatī payasvinī gāndhārī pūṣā śaṅkhinī sarasvatī iḍā piṅgalā suṣumnā ceti caturdaśa nāḍyaḥ || 12 || sarva-saṃkṣobhiṇī ādi caturdaśāragā devatāḥ || 13 || prāṇa-apāna-vyāna-udāna-samāna-nāga-kūrma-kṛkara-devadatta-dhanañjayā iti daśa vāyavaḥ | sarva-siddhipradādi bahirdaśāragā devatāḥ || 14 || etad vāyu-daśakaḥ saṃsargopādhibhedhena recaka-pācaka-śoṣaka-dāhaka-plāvakā amṛtamiti prāṇamukhyatvena pañcadhā jaṭhara-agnirbhavati | kṣāraka udgārakaḥ kṣobhako mohako jṛmbhaka iti nāga-prādhānyena pañcavidho'sti | tena manuṣyāṇāṃ dehānāṃ bhakṣya-bhojya-coṣya-lehya-peyātmakaṃ pañcavidham-annaṃ pācayanti | etā daśa vahnikalāḥ sarvajñādyā antardaśāragā devatāḥ || 15 || śīta-uṣṇa-sukha-duḥkha-icchāḥ sattva-rajas-tamoguṇā vaśinī ādi śaktayo'ṣṭau || 16 || śabda-sparśa-rūpa-rasa-gandhā× pañca-tanmātrā× pañca-puṣpabāṇāḥ | mana ikṣu-dhanuḥ | rāga× pāśaḥ | dveṣo'ṅkuśaḥ || 17 || avyakta-mahattattvam-mahadahaṅkārāḥ iti kāmeśvarī-vajreśvarī-bhagamālinyantas trikoṇāgragā devatāḥ || 18 || nirupādhikā saṃvideva kāmeśvaraḥ | sadānandapūrṇā svātmaiva paradevatā lalitā | lauhityametasya sarvasya vimarśaḥ || 19 || ananyacittatvena

ca siddhiḥ || 20 || bhāvanāyā× kriyā upacārāḥ | ahaṃ tvam
asti nāsti kartavyam akartavyam upāsitavyam iti vikalpānām
ātmani vilāpanaṃ homaḥ | bhāvanā viṣayāṇām abheda-
bhāvanā tarpaṇam || 21 || pañcadaśa tithi-rūpeṇa kālasya
pariṇāmā avalokanaṃ pañcadaśa nityāḥ || 22 || evaṃ
muhūrta-tritayaṃ muhūrta-dvitayaṃ muhūrta-mātraṃ vā
bhāvanāparo jīvanmukto bhavati | sa eva śivayogī iti gadyate
|| 23 || kādimatena antaścakra-bhāvanā× pratipāditāḥ || 24 ||
ya evaṃ veda | saḥ atharvaśiraḥ adhīte || 25 || ityupaniṣat ||

oṃ bhadraṃ karṇebhiḥ śṛṇuyāma devāḥ | bhadraṃ paśye
mākṣabhir yajatrāḥ | sthirairaṅgais tuṣṭuvāṃ sastanūbhiḥ |
vyaśema devahitaṃ yadāyuḥ || svasti na indro vṛddhaśravāḥ
| svasti naḥ pūṣā viśvavedāḥ | svasti nastārkṣyo ariṣṭanemiḥ
| svasti no bṛhaspatirdadhātu || oṃ śāntiḥ śāntiḥ śāntiḥ ||

Sanskrit Grammar

Sandhis separated word by word पदच्छेद (प॰),
and with विभक्ति Cases have been listed.

<u>Abbreviations</u>
Nouns

    m masculine, **f** feminine, **n** neuter; **V** vocative
    1/1 = vibhakti from 1 to 7/number 1 to 3
    adj = adjective, adv = adverb

Indeclinables (uninflected nouns or verbs) **0.**
In Sanskrit the **adverbs** are mostly uninflected.
Adjective follows a Substantive in case and number.

Verbs

    iii/1 = person i to iii / number 1 to 3
    PPP = Past Participle Passive = क्त
    PPA = Past Participle Active = क्तवत्
    PrPA = Present Participle Active = शतृ / शानच्
    FPA = Future Participle Active = लृट् + शतृ
    PoPP = Potential Participle Passive = य, तव्य, अनीयर्
    (gerundive)

It is a common practice in Sanskrit grammar to use a
"hyphen" to indicate compounds.
Compound or समास is frequently encountered in Sanskrit
literature. It has a beauty and a brevity.

Since Sanskrit is an inflectional language, the **spelling of the same word** changes as per context or usage. Hence words can be **placed anywhere** in a sentence, as in poetic use, without change in meaning. The matrix shows how.

Verb inflections in Sanskrit – a sample chart

982 गम्ऌ गतौ – to go, also in the sense of attainment			
Present Tense Active voice लट् कर्त्तरि			
Person/no	singular	dual	plural
Third	गच्छति iii/1	गच्छतः iii/2	गच्छन्ति iii/3
Second	गच्छसि ii/1	गच्छथः ii/2	गच्छथ ii/3
First	गच्छामि i/1	गच्छावः i/2	गच्छामः i/3

Noun declensions in Sanskrit – a sample chart

Masculine stem, vowel अ ending			
(रू–आ–म्–अ) राम m Lord's name			
	singular [1]	dual [2]	plural [3]
1 Doer	रामः 1/1	रामौ 1/2	रामाः 1/3
2 Object	रामम् 2/1	रामौ 2/2	रामान् 2/3
3 by	रामेण 3/1	रामाभ्याम् 3/2	रामैः 3/3
4 for	रामाय 4/1	रामाभ्याम् 4/2	रामेभ्यः 4/3
5 from	रामात् 5/1	रामाभ्याम् 5/2	रामेभ्यः 5/3
6 of	रामस्य 6/1	रामयोः 6/2	रामाणाम् 6/3
7 in	रामे 7/1	रामयोः 7/2	रामेषु 7/3
Vocative	हे राम V/1	हे रामौ V/2	हे रामाः V/3

Masculine stem, consonant त् ending

मरुत् [m] Wind, Breeze, Air			
	singular [1]	dual [2]	plural [3]
1 Doer	मरुत् [1/1]	मरुतौ [1/2]	मरुतः [1/3]
2 Object	मरुतम् [2/1]	मरुतौ [2/2]	मरुतः [2/3]
3 by	मरुता [3/1]	मरुद्भ्याम् [3/2]	मरुद्भिः [3/3]
4 for	मरुते [4/1]	मरुद्भ्याम् [4/2]	मरुद्भ्यः [4/3]
5 from	मरुतः [5/1]	मरुद्भ्याम् [5/2]	मरुद्भ्यः [5/3]
6 of	मरुतः [6/1]	मरुतोः [6/2]	मरुताम् [6/3]
7 in	मरुति [7/1]	मरुतोः [7/2]	मरुत्सु [7/3]
Vocative	हे मरुत् [V/1]	हे मरुतौ [V/2]	हे मरुतः [V/3]

Moods and Tenses in Sanskrit

1	लट्	Present Tense
2	लुङ्	Aorist Past Tense, before from now
3	लङ्	Imperfect Past Tense – before from yesterday onwards
4	लिट्	Perfect Past Tense – distant unseen past
5	लृट्	Simple Future Tense – now onwards
6	लुट्	Periphrastic Future Tense – tomorrow onwards
7	लृङ्	Conditional Mood - if/then, past or future
8	लोट्	Imperative Mood – request
9	विधि॰	Potential Mood – order विधिलिङ्
10	आशिर्	Benedictive Mood – blessing आशीर्लिङ् (also used in the sense of a curse)

Conjugation process of Verb

अधीते ^{लट्} iii/1 = she/he learns with dedication

from Upasarga अधि + Root 1046 √ इङ् अध्ययने । 2cA

1.3.1 भूवादयो धातवः । इङ्

1.3.3 हलन्त्यम् । 1.3.9 तस्य लोपः । इ

3.4.69 लः कर्मणि च भावे चाकर्मकेभ्यः । इ

3.2.123 वर्तमाने लट् । 3.4.77 लस्य । इ + लँट्

1.3.3 हलन्त्यम् । 1.3.9 तस्य लोपः । इ + लँ

1.3.2 उपदेशोऽजनुनासिक इत् । 1.3.9 तस्य लोपः । इ + ल्

3.4.78 तिप्तस्झिसिप्थस्थमिब्वस्मस् तातांझथासाथांध्वमिड्वहिमहिङ् ।

Atmanepada इ + तातांझ । conjugating third person

1.4.101 तिङस्त्रीणि त्रीणि प्रथममध्यमोत्तमाः ।

1.4.102 तान्येकवचनद्विवचनबहुवचनान्येकशः । इ + त । singular

1.4.108 शेषे प्रथमः । known as Prathma Purusha

3.4.113 तिङ्शित्सार्वधातुकम् । इ + त

3.1.68 कर्तरि शप् । 2.4.72 अदिप्रभृतिभ्यः शपः । इ + त

3.4.79 टित आत्मनेपदानां टेरे । इ + ते ।

1.2.4 सार्वधातुकमपित् । इ + ते । = इते ^{लट्} iii/1 । She studies

    With Upasarga अधि + इते 6.1.101 अकः सवर्णे दीर्घः । =

    अधीते ^{लट्} iii/1 । She studies devotedly. She masters.

Declension process of Noun

ललिता = Playful Goddess, Glow of Light, Sweet and Bright
Stem ललिता f → ललिता f 1/1

1.2.45 अर्थवदधातुरप्रत्ययः प्रातिपदिकम् । ललिता

1.2.46 कृत्तद्धितसमासाश्च । 3.1.1 प्रत्ययः । 3.1.2 परश्च ।

4.1.1 ङ्याप्प्रातिपदिकात्

4.1.2 स्वौजस-

    मौट्छष्टाभ्याम्भिस्ङेभ्याम्भ्यस्ङसिभ्याम्भ्यस्ङसोसाम्ङ्योस्सुप् ।

1.4.104 विभक्तिश्च । 1.4.103 सुपः = use one of these vibhakti
suffix. ललिता + सुँ ।

1.4.22 ब्येकयोर्द्विवचनैकवचने = singular number taken.

    ललिता + सुँ $^{1/1}$ ।

1.3.2 उपदेशेऽजनुनासिक इत् । 1.3.9 तस्य लोपः । ललिता + स् ।

6.1.68 हल्ङ्याब्भ्यो दीर्घात् सुतिस्यपृक्तं हल् । ललिता ।

    = ललिता $^{f1/1}$ । *Feminine. First case singular.*

Playful Enchanting Charming Goddess. Attractive Light.
Delightful form. Evoking Sweetness. Giving Protection.

Sanskrit Alphabet and Principles in Creation

The Sanskrit Alphabet

SN	Unicode of Transliterated text	Latin	Devanagari	Remarks
1	0061	a	अ	Short vowel ह्रस्व स्वर time duration 1 units
2	0101	ā	आ	Long vowel दीर्घ स्वर time duration 2 units
3	0069	i	इ	Short vowel ह्रस्व स्वर time duration 1 units
4	012B	ī	ई	Long vowel दीर्घ स्वर time duration 2 units
5	0075	u	उ	Short vowel ह्रस्व स्वर time duration 1 units
6	016B	ū	ऊ	Long vowel दीर्घ स्वर time duration 2 units
7	1E5B	ṛ	ऋ	Short vowel ह्रस्व स्वर time duration 1 units
8	1E5D	ṝ	ॠ	Long vowel दीर्घ स्वर time duration 2 units
9	1E37	ḷ	ळ	Short vowel ह्रस्व स्वर time duration 1 units
10	0065	e	ए	(Diphthong) Compound vowel सन्धि अक्षर duration 2 units
11	0061+0069	ai	ऐ	(Diphthong) Compound vowel सन्धि अक्षर duration 2 units

12	006F	o	ओ	(Diphthong) Compound vowel सन्धि अक्षर duration 2 units
13	0061+ 0075	au	औ	(Diphthong) Compound vowel सन्धि अक्षर duration 2 units
14	0061+ 1E43	aṃ	अं (अ ◌ं)	Ayogavaha अयोगवाह having characteristics of vowel and consonant both (अम्)
15	0061+1E2 5	aḥ	अः (अ ◌:)	Ayogavaha अयोगवाह having characteristics of vowel and consonant both (अह्)
16	006B	k	क्	Consonant व्यञ्जन time duration ½ unit
17	006B+ 0068	kh	ख्	Consonant व्यञ्जन time duration ½ unit
18	0067	g	ग्	Consonant व्यञ्जन time duration ½ unit
19	0067+ 0068	gh	घ्	Consonant व्यञ्जन time duration ½ unit
20	1E45	ṅ	ङ्	Consonant व्यञ्जन time duration ½ unit
21	0063	c	च्	Consonant व्यञ्जन time duration ½ unit
22	0063+ 0068	ch	छ्	Consonant व्यञ्जन time duration ½ unit
23	006A	j	ज्	Consonant व्यञ्जन time duration ½ unit

24	006A+ 0068	jh	झ़	Consonant व्यञ्जन time duration ½ unit
25	00F1	ñ	ञ़	Consonant व्यञ्जन time duration ½ unit
26	1E6D	ṭ	ट़	Consonant व्यञ्जन time duration ½ unit
27	1E6D+ 0068	ṭh	ठ़	Consonant व्यञ्जन time duration ½ unit
28	1E0D	ḍ	ड़	Consonant व्यञ्जन time duration ½ unit
29	1E0D+ 0068	ḍh	ढ़	Consonant व्यञ्जन time duration ½ unit
30	1E47	ṇ	ण़	Consonant व्यञ्जन time duration ½ unit
31	0074	t	त़	Consonant व्यञ्जन time duration ½ unit
32	0074+ 0068	th	थ़	Consonant व्यञ्जन time duration ½ unit
33	0064	d	द़	Consonant व्यञ्जन time duration ½ unit
34	0064+ 0068	dh	ध़	Consonant व्यञ्जन time duration ½ unit
35	006E	n	ऩ	Consonant व्यञ्जन time duration ½ unit
36	0070	p	प़	Consonant व्यञ्जन time duration ½ unit
37	0070+ 0068	ph	फ़	Consonant व्यञ्जन time duration ½ unit
38	0062	b	ब़	Consonant व्यञ्जन time duration ½ unit

39	0062+ 0068	bh	भ्	Consonant व्यञ्जन time duration ½ unit
40	006D	m	म्	Consonant व्यञ्जन time duration ½ unit
41	0079	y	य्	Consonant व्यञ्जन time duration ½ unit
42	0072	r	र्	Consonant व्यञ्जन time duration ½ unit
43	006C	l	ल्	Consonant व्यञ्जन time duration ½ unit
44	0076	v	व्	Consonant व्यञ्जन time duration ½ unit
45	015B	ś	श्	Consonant व्यञ्जन time duration ½ unit
46	1E63	ṣ	ष्	Consonant व्यञ्जन time duration ½ unit
47	0073	s	स्	Consonant व्यञ्जन time duration ½ unit
48	0068	h	ह्	Consonant व्यञ्जन time duration ½ unit
49	013C	ḷ	ळ्	Consonant व्यञ्जन time duration ½ unit
Unicode without Transliteration				
50	0905+0969	अ३	अ३	(Protracted) Pluta Vowel प्लुत time duration 3 units
51	0907+0969	इ३	इ३	(Protracted) Pluta Vowel प्लुत time duration 3 units
52	0909+0969	उ३	उ३	(Protracted) Pluta Vowel प्लुत time duration 3 units
53	090B+	ऋ३	ऋ३	(Protracted) Pluta Vowel

	0969			झुत time duration 3 units
54	090C+ 0969	लृ३	लृ३	(Protracted) Pluta Vowel झुत time duration 3 units
55	090F+ 0969	ए३	ए३	(Protracted) Pluta Vowel झुत time duration 3 units
56	0913+ 0969	ओ३	ओ३	(Protracted) Pluta Vowel झुत time duration 3 units

Sanskrit Alphabet Extended to account for Principles in Creation

57	1E39	Ī	लॢ	Long Vowel दीर्घ स्वर time duration 2 units
58	006B+1E 63+0061	kṣa	क्ष	Immutable Supreme Soul कूटस्थ

Unicode Character Sets in Use

Basic Latin	0020 to 007E
Latin-1 Supplement	00A0 to 00FF
Latin Extended-A	0100 to 017F
Latin Extended-B	0180 to 0217
Devanagari	0901 to 0970
Latin Extended Additional	1E00 to 1EF9

36 Principles in Creation

SN	Seed Sound	Principle
1	कं	Earth पृथिवी solid mass
2	खं	Water आपः liquid matter
3	गं	Fire अग्नि glowing matter
4	घं	Air वायु effervescent matter
5	ङं	Space आकाश invisible unmeasurable
6	चं	Smell घ्राण the function of earth
7	छं	Taste रस the function of water
8	जं	Sight दृष्टि form the function of fire
9	झं	Touch स्पर्श the attribute of air
10	ञं	Sound शब्द attribute of space
11	टं	anus पायु organ of elimination
12	ठं	penis उपस्थ organ of reproduction
13	डं	hands पाणी organ of grasping
14	ढं	feet पादौ organ of locomotion
15	णं	speech वाक् organ of sound
16	तं	nose घ्राण sense organ of smell
17	थं	tongue जिह्वा sense organ of taste
18	दं	eyes चक्षुस् sense organ of sight
19	धं	skin त्वक् sense organ of touch
20	नं	ears श्रोत्रम् sense organ of hearing
21	पं	nature प्रकृति primordial nature
22	फं	ego अहङ्कार notion of mineness

23	बं	intellect बुद्धि reasoning and decision
24	भं	mind मनस् controller of senses and thought producer
25	मं	Jiva soul पुरुष individual being
26	यं	Marking कला raw unprocessed touch
27	रं	Information अल्पज्ञता raw unprocessed sight
28	लं	Attachment राग raw unprocessed smell
29	वं	Time काल raw unprocessed flow
30	ळं	Event नियति raw unprocessed emptiness
31	शं	Purity शुद्ध विद्या divine expression
32	षं	Force ईश्वर raw strength
33	सं	Eternal Force सदाशिव
34	हं	Shakti शक्ति universal power and energy
35	क्षं	Shiva शिव which holds power and energy
36	अं	Spark ब्रह्मन् Brahman that enables all

References

https://www.ashtangayoga.info/philosophy/sanskrit-and-devanagari/transliteration-tool/
https://www.learnsanskrit.cc/

https://manblunder.com/articles/sri-chakra-articles

Bhavanopanishad Chant and explanation
https://www.youtube.com/watch?v=zHLQP6mogB4
Srimadh Lalita Maha Tripurasundari Devasthanam
http://www.slmt.co.in/Home/Navaavaranam

S. Subhramanya Sastri, T. R. Srinivasa Ayyangar –Saundarya Lahiri - 1st – 1948 – The Theosophical Publishing House, Adyar, Madras.

S. K. Ramachandra Rao – The Tantra of Sri Chakra (Bhavanopanishat) - 1st – 1983 –Sharada Prakashana, Bangalore.

Rajendra Ranjan Chaturvedi – श्रीविद्या कल्पलता - 1st – 1998 – Motilal Banarsidass, Delhi.

Sri Sivananda, Krishnanand Budhauliya – श्रीमातृकाचक्र विवेकः – 2nd – 1998 – Sripitambara Pitha Sanskrit Parishad, Datia, Madhya Pradesh.

Sri Karapatra Swami, Sri Sitarama Kaviraja – श्रीविद्यारलाकरः - 8th – 2012 – Srividya Sadhana Pitha, Varanasi.

Ashwini Kumar Aggarwal – Sri Yantra with Golden Ratio Triangle and Inscriptions – 1st – 2023 – Devotees of Sri Sri Ravi Shankar Ashram, Punjab.

Epilogue

Sing freely.
Sing from your Soul.
Sing whenever you want.

Offer all to Her and rest deeply.

सर्वे भवन्तु सुखिनः । सर्वे सन्तु निरामयाः ।

सर्वे भद्राणि पश्यन्तु । मा कश्चिद् दुःख भाग् भवेत् ॥

ॐ शान्तिः शान्तिः शान्तिः ॥

When faith has blossomed in life,
Every step is led by the Divine.

Sri Sri Ravi Shankar

Om Namah Shivaya

जय गुरुदेव

www.ingramcontent.com/pod-product-compliance
Lightning Source LLC
Chambersburg PA
CBHW020742160726
47993CB00006B/2579